The Countryside our Classroom

A Cotswold village school in the 1960s

Gordon Ottewell

GORDON OTTEWELL

Barn Owl Books

Copyright 2009 by Gordon Ottewell.

Published by Barn Owl Books,
33 Delavale Road, Winchcombe, Cheltenham,
Gloucestershire. GL54 5YL, United Kingdom.
Tel. 01242 603464.

Printing by SS-Media Ltd.

Typesetting and production by Robert Talbot, to whom
the author is greatly indebted.

British Library Cataloguing in Publication Data.
A catalogue record for this book is available from the
British Library.
ISBN 978-0-9510586-8-8

Introduction

In 1964, as a comparatively young teacher taking charge of a village school set deep in the Cotswold countryside, it seemed logical to base much of my teaching on the local environment, or as the modern phrase goes, 'the great outdoors.' I have no evidence whatever to suggest that the children I taught have as a result led more fulfilling lives than their contemporaries elsewhere; all I know is that together we shared countless happy and enriching learning experiences in the fields and woods, along the hedgerows and by the waterside, around the village and further afield.

This little book is predominantly a light hearted account of those seven years spent as a full-time teaching head. They were by far my most satisfying years in the profession. I was privileged to be able to lead my school according to my personal beliefs in a way that is unthinkable today.

Among the store of happy memories of those faraway days, one in particular comes to mind. We were walking along a wide stretch of coast path during a field trip in Somerset. After a day spent on intensive fieldwork, followed by the recording of our findings in the hostel workroom, we were taking an evening stroll before bedtime when a girl broke the brief silence.
    'I wish we could go on like this for ever.'
Such rewards repay a teacher's efforts a thousand fold.

Gordon Ottewell
Winchcombe
August 2009

Children, 1967.

The Countryside Our Classroom

Chapter 1

On a grey Friday afternoon in January 1957, I cycled out of the gates of a Derbyshire colliery yard for the last time. After almost ten years spent as a surveyor's assistant underground, I was about to embark on a teaching career, having been offered a place in a training college for the following September. In the meantime, the local education office had agreed to employ me in a temporary capacity in a large junior school in a nearby village, which I had visited briefly after work a short time earlier.

I began my spell of unqualified teaching on the following Monday. It was a raw, bleak winter morning. The grim walled playground, deserted on my previous visit, was now engulfed by a tide of racing, raucous children, none of whom paid the slightest heed to the young man self-consciously pushing his bike towards the staff cycle shed.

The head teacher, looking if possible even more careworn than on my earlier visit, extricated himself from behind a desk piled high with books and papers and led the way through waves of children towards a distant temporary-looking building not included in my earlier visit. Following on his heels, I strained to catch his words above the incessant din.

' ….. first years to start with…… 1A, then 1B……. couple of weeks with each……. Mrs Burgin…… took some persuading, believe me……. Not the easiest, as you'll discover….. Anyway, see how you get on.'

We got no further than the door. A tall, bony woman, hair swept back severely, face an ashen mask, blocked our path. The words, terse and strident, erupted above the babble. 'I'm sorry, Mr

5

Pickering, but I can't! I haven't slept a wink all weekend – sick with worry. I've talked it through with Harry and he agrees. I'm sorry, but the very idea of having someone – '.

I quickly sidestepped and hovered at a distance, awaiting the outcome. Not the best of starts but surely things would get better – wouldn't they?

A frowning Mr Pickering made his way towards me through the milling throng, his eyes avoiding my enquiring gaze.

'Hmm, unfortunate that - very unfortunate,' he mumbled miserably. 'Thought I'd got her to agree to you starting with her - but no. Bit of a law unto herself, I'm afraid.' I became aware of a facial twitch. 'And her sister's much the same – she takes 3A. We'll get the same response there too, if I'm not mistaken.' He gave a weak, unhappy grin. 'Oh well, we'd better try 1B – Miss May. She's not expecting you for a fortnight but I'm sure she'll understand.' He led the way to the adjoining room.

Miss May assured us she *did* understand. Slight, youthful - a tiny face, bird-like behind thick glasses - she broke off from her purposeful bustling to proffer a welcoming hand. The relief on Mr Pickering's face was momentarily ecstatic. Then he was off through the door in an instant.

The two weeks with 1B flew by. Miss May enthused. More than that, she positively bubbled. I watched in wonder as this tiny woman, faced with a class of thirty or more seven-year-olds ranging from the noisy and ill-disciplined to the timid and withdrawn, somehow managed to communicate her obvious delight in life to her charges and in so doing made the process of learning – whether it be language or number, nature, art, physical education or music – an absorbing and thoroughly enjoyable experience.

Which was more than could be said for most of the teaching I witnessed over the following months. Excluded, as Mr Pickering had predicted, not only from Mrs Burgin's class but also from that of her unsmiling spinster sister, my experience was limited to six streamed classes, plus one remedial class spanning several age groups, taught by a rotund elderly lady for whom the adjective formidable could well have been coined, and housed in yet another remotely-sited building on the far side of the playground.

Working my way through the classes, I arrived eventually at 3B, that of a comparatively young male teacher, whose well-dressed appearance and caustic staffroom asides defied the tweedy-weedy-seedy image to which male teachers were supposed to conform. On first entering this classroom and seeing every window sill crammed with plant pots and boxes of seedlings, I assumed that here was a teacher with a particular interest in rural studies. However, my remarks to this effect were greeted with a hollow laugh.

'Rural studies? Heavens, no! The plants are mine. These windows catch the sun better than any greenhouse. You should have seen the crop of tomatoes I grew last year.' He nodded towards the children, impassive in their desks. 'I have to watch the little devils, though – one or two of them are not above helping themselves.' Art, I was to discover, was Mr Collins's speciality. Or rather, every afternoon was devoted to what he termed 'free expression.' The routine seldom varied. A select little group of girls dutifully covered the desks with old newspapers before giving out paper, paint, brushes and water. Mr Collins, meanwhile, chalked up three suggested titles on the blackboard, along the lines of:

A farmyard
Ships at sea
A busy street

Then, for the benefit of non-readers, he read out the choices, made it clear that he was not to be disturbed until break time, and settled back at his desk to polish off any marking or to read his newspaper. Occasionally, a child would approach the desk, hold-

7

ing a dripping picture for inspection.

'Please sir, I've finished.'

'Finished? Of course you haven't – nowhere near. Put in some clouds.'

'But it's supposed to be a storm, sir. There ain't no clouds.'

'Well – put in some birds, then. Or a sinking ship – or something. There's twenty minutes to go yet.'

One afternoon, feeling superfluous, I wandered round the room, watching the children at work and offering words of encouragement before returning to the front of the class. 'That's a nasty blob of paint on your jacket,' Mr Collins observed, looking up from his paper. 'I used to get within splashing distance at one time. Soon learnt my lesson though. They know that they mustn't bring their daubs any nearer than that.' He pointed to a line chalked on the floor in front of his desk.

After sitting through one of Mr Collins's history lessons on the Saxon period, which consisted of reading round the class from a set of dog-eared textbooks left behind from an earlier age, I ventured to suggest a class visit to the site of a Norman castle, barely a mile from the school. Mr Collins frowned. Too far to walk, he explained, and not far enough to hire a bus. And although he had never been there, he understood that virtually no trace remained and what little could be seen stood on private land, to which access could be a problem. At this point Mr Collins delivered his trump card. The weather, he reminded me, could well prove uncooperative at this time of year. And so, much as he welcomed my interest, he was sure I would appreciate that such a departure from the timetable couldn't be justified. Perhaps later in the year, then, I suggested. Again, the frown. The Normans would be over and done with by then. I gave up.

The following weekend, after reading about the castle's eventful history in the local library, I approached the farmer on whose land it stood. Permission to visit the site was readily given and I was able to bring away a few examples of roofing tiles and other remains. Mr Collins buried his head in his marking while the children eagerly examined these and listened attentively as I gave a brief account of the part the castle played in the neighbourhood in Norman times.

Apart from the effervescent Miss May, the only other teacher who seemed to enjoy her work was Mrs Gingell, the deputy head, a heavily-built, florid-faced woman nearing retirement, who taught the fourth-year A -stream class. It was my good fortune to spend my last few weeks at the school in her classroom, for although she prided herself in being one of 'the old school', and professed to having no time for 'so-called modern methods', there was no disputing her ability at bringing out the best in her children, while at the same time commanding their respect, and for all her firmness, their affection.

With the summer holiday beckoning, to be followed by transfer to their respective secondary schools, these children were naturally high-spirited. Even so, they listened in rapt concentration as Mrs Gingell read the final chapters of *The Pilgrim's Progress*, a book she shared with every class during their final term and from which she extracted every ounce of meaning from the familiar text.

As the last few weeks of term ebbed away, Mrs Gingell agreed to my request to be allowed to lead a nature ramble along the towpath of the abandoned canal close to the school. We had not gone far when this remarkable teacher began to reveal her extensive knowledge of wild flowers and soon all the girls and a few of the boys were gathered around her as she identified various species and explained their differing life cycles.

Rashly, I suggested taking the remaining boys further along the towpath to see the hulk of a partly submerged narrow boat. All went well until we rounded a bend and their teacher was out of sight. Suddenly, as though responding to a prearranged signal and totally ignoring my pleas to stop, they broke into a run, leaving me alone and helpless. I suspect they learned very little from their walk: I, on the other hand, learned a valuable lesson the hard way.

The last day of term arrived and I took my leave of Mr Pickering in his poky, cluttered office. I had seen virtually nothing of him during my six months at his school and conversation was as stilted now as on our first meeting. His response to my expression of gratitude for the experience gained was guarded.

'I expect you'll come out of college full of fancy ideas.' I looked in vain for a twinkle of the eye. 'We all did – but very few of them stand the test of time. Anyway, good luck.'

Cycling homeward along the canal towpath, where my recent unhappy experience had taken place, I pondered on Mr Pickering's uninspiring words. Would I too, in time, become a cynic, seeing teaching as a joyless chore? Surely not, with the likes of the youthful Miss May and the mature Mrs Gingell on whom to base my ideals.

Chapter 2

Following my marriage, and an idyllic honeymoon spent in the heart of the Quantock Hills in Somerset, I commenced my teacher training at Worcester, a college to which I had been strongly advised to apply on account of its high reputation for rural and environmental studies facilities. This meant that my wife and I were compelled to live apart during term time – by no means an ideal arrangement but one that proved unavoidable. To my relief, I discovered that the year's intake included a handful of other mature students, some of whom shared my own particular circumstances. In fact, a few of the friendships that were established at that time have survived through to the present day.

The most valuable part of the college experience was without doubt the four spells of teaching practice. Varying in duration from two to four weeks, they provided the opportunity to participate, albeit briefly, in the life of widely contrasting schools. These ranged from a tiny school set in a picture-postcard village, presided over by an elderly headmistress by whom the cane and the punishment book were put to daily use for the most trivial of offences, to a lively city-fringe school, which despite its antiquated buildings, gave out a welcoming feel that reflected the enlightened attitude of the forward-thinking headmaster.

It was in this school that I was based for my final practice, teaching a bubbly class of top juniors. I had been studying the behaviour of tawny owls in the college grounds and had collected a number of pellets in which the birds regurgitated the indigestible bones and fur of their prey. The head readily agreed to my suggestion of a project on birds of prey, which culminated in each child being given a pellet to dissect and being required to report on its contents. The project proved a great success and brought the practice to a happy conclusion.

It was my good fortune to have as one of my tutors, Frederick Grice, author of several highly regarded children's books, including *The Bonnie Pit Laddie*. He was a native of Durham and our shared affinity with mining folk gave rise to what for me was much valued discussion. Towards the end of my course, Mr Grice introduced a small group of us to William Plomer, who in 1938 had been responsible for bringing to light the diaries of Francis Kilvert, the Wiltshire-born clergyman, whose descriptions of life in and around the Welsh borderland village of Clyro in Victorian times had become something of a literary classic. I knew nothing of the man or of his diaries but as a result of Plomer's brief address, at the earliest opportunity I borrowed a fellow student's bicycle and set off one free weekend to see for myself the village that the young curate had immortalised. It was not until many years later, on discovering by chance a copy of his valuable book, *Francis Kilvert and his World*, that I learned that Frederick Grice was himself a leading authority on the celebrated diarist.

Worcester in the late 1950s had yet to suffer the mindless vandalism that was soon to be inflicted on its ancient streets and their irreplaceable old buildings. Among these, a fellow book lover and I came upon a run-down second hand establishment which rewarded our browsing by yielding what seemed an unlimited supply of collectable books on natural history and topography at near giveaway prices. Thanks to this discovery, I was able to add to my modest library a motley mix of the works of among others, Richard Jefferies, W.H. Hudson, Henry Thoreau and several lesser-known authors, all of whom contributed to my growing interest in the natural world.

A fellow member of the college naturalists' society, also a mature student, lived with his teacher wife in a caravan in a delectable corner of Worcestershire merely a few miles from college. Thanks to regular weekend visits, I became acquainted with this richly varied landscape of field, woodland and ancient rambling hedges, alongside which quiet bridleways and footpaths picked their way. Here I became familiar with several summer visiting birds – garden and wood warbler, lesser whitethroat, spotted flycatcher – which I had failed to record further north, as well as a whole range of flowering plants entirely new to me. Like me, my friend had embarked on a teaching career through dissatisfaction with work in industry and was determined to succeed in this new venture. He too experienced extreme contrasts in the atmosphere of the schools in which he served his teaching practices and in the attitude of the teachers he encountered. Together, we found it incomprehensible that some members of the profession to which we aspired to belong seemed to regard teaching merely as just another job. In my case, after having squandered almost ten years of my life as a misfit – a square peg down the round hole of a coal mine – success in my new career was in every sense absolutely vital.

My two years at Worcester sped by. Elected as president of the student body in my second year, I was called upon to officiate at various college events, including the visit of the minister for education. And although I savoured every moment, devoting all my time and energy to college life and work, I never lost sight of the twin goals I had set myself – to qualify at the highest possible level and to obtain a post in a progressive village school in my native Derbyshire.

To my relief, I achieved the first of these goals, with distinctions in all subjects, including the all-important one of practical teaching. I was now equipped to make my way in the profession. I couldn't wait to begin. It only remained to secure my first appointment.

We had set our hearts on making our home in the Dove valley and midway through my second year at college we were overjoyed to obtain a house in a secluded position in our chosen area. Our delight proved to be short lived, however, for having no car and with no bus route near, my scope in searching for a suitable vacancy was severely limited. In fact, there were no posts to be had whatever. Margaret fared better; her secretarial skills promptly secured her a job in mill offices within an easy cycle ride of home.

At length, after combing through the national vacancy lists with growing anxiety, I came across a vacancy for a teacher of general subjects at a small newly-opened secondary modern school in Staffordshire, some ten miles from home, and to my relief was appointed. Fortunately too, I was granted permission to travel on the school bus, which ran from a nearby village over the county boundary. It was not exactly the kind of start to my teaching career that I had intended but at least I had a job, and in a country school.

The two years I spent teaching older children proved to be a valuable experience. Despite the inflexible timetabling, which meant a line of new faces outside my door every forty minutes, I enjoyed my English, history and geography lessons, especially with the lower forms. Selection at eleven-plus had quite unjustly branded these children as failures and while by no means all were academically endowed, I soon discovered that a good number, self-conscious and apprehensive at first in their pristine new blazers, possessed considerable ability and responded readily to enthusiastic teaching.

The one drawback to travelling to and from school by bus was that the arrangement allowed too little time for morning preparation, end-of-day marking and general self – evaluation. This meant that these essential activities had to be crammed into the lunchtime break, together with staff meetings, mounting displays and running a nature club, which provided a valuable means of getting to know a small group of children informally, away from the constraints of the restrictive timetable. Although most of the club members were first years, as yet unaffected by the adolescent traits displayed by the older children, the club attracted a few teenagers, one of whom, a farmer's son, responded to my appeal for specimens of abandoned nests and relatively intact bird road casualties by rummaging in his pocket to produce a duck's foot, salvaged from the previous day's dinner.

Teaching the older children proved a sterner challenge. For some reason, social studies for the upper forms was organised on a single-sex basis. This worked well enough with the senior boys; working on the principle 'Teach what you know best', I was able to arrange a visit, including an underground tour, to a colliery, which proved to be an exciting experience for them and a strangely nostalgic one for me. Faced with a group of senior girls, however, I soon found that my primary –stage training left me woefully ill-equipped. Sensing that their teacher, though not perhaps still in the full flush of youth, was nevertheless a raw beginner, a minority were quick to exploit my inexperience and it took the combined efforts of some of the more mature members of the group to per-suade the troublemakers to ease the pressure on their rookie teacher.

Concerned at my inability to control this unruly element, let alone teach them effectively, I confided in the elderly rural science teacher with whom I travelled on the school bus. He gave a know-ing chuckle. 'Those lasses can't wait to leave – to shake off school and everything it stands for,' he said. 'All they want is to get a job – any job – and earn money. You're in your probationary year. Your job is to survive. As it is, they see you as part of the system. You've got to show them that, despite that, you're on their side – or at least as much as you can be.' He went on to relate how he had overheard some of these girls discussing how a female mem-ber of staff, a probationer like myself, made a habit of undoing the top button of her blouse when taking a class of senior boys. 'And they were right!' he added. 'I hadn't noticed before but they miss nothing. Truth be known, some of them are more worldly wise than she is, for all her college poise.'

15

I thanked him for his advice. Wisdom, worldly or otherwise, I reflected, was not the exclusive monopoly of the educated and mature.

Although I found the work reasonably rewarding, I never lost sight of my original aim to teach in the primary field. But with opportunities few and far between locally, it was clear that to obtain a post in a progressive school I would need to travel. And to travel I would need my own transport. Buying a small, inexpensive car was easily done; qualifying to drive it was another matter entirely. Cars – apart from the 'Dinky' variety of my childhood – have never remotely interested me and now, despite having taken lessons, the presence of a silent, hawk-eyed examiner by my side unnerved me to such an extent that I failed my test twice and sold the car in despair. In the meantime, I had successfully applied for a post in a large go-ahead junior school almost twenty miles distant. How on earth, I asked myself, would I get there?

The answer was – with difficulty. The only way possible was to walk two miles to a remote bus stop for a fifteen-mile journey into Derby, then change buses for another three-mile ride to the school, reversing the process at the day's end. In good weather, the walking was both enjoyable and health-promoting; on wet days something of an ordeal. But with a lively class of third-year juniors, working under a sympathetic if somewhat idiosyncratic head, every day was a new adventure, to be savoured to the full, and the twice-daily journeys, time-consuming though they were, seemed a small price to pay for such an opportunity.

Home life, meanwhile, more than lived up to our fondest hopes. There was always plenty to do in our larger-than-average garden; we rejoiced in having fields and woods as our immediate neighbours, and thanks to the friendly tenant of a nearby farm, I was able to enjoy exclusive rights to watch a thriving badger set, spending many an evening observing the occupants foraging for food, playing king-of-the-castle and generally going about their lives oblivious to my presence on a sheltered tree-stump close by. That spring too, we added a new bird to our list. Working in the garden one evening, we heard an unfamiliar whistling sound overhead, followed immediately by a low croak. Looking up, we spotted a squat, long-billed bird beating its way over the trees and realised that for the first time in our lives we were witnessing the roding flight of the male woodcock. From then on, watching this unique spectacle became a dusk ritual, one which we delighted in sharing with visiting friends.

But a combination of changing circumstances were about to bring our all-too-brief rural idyll to an end. Somewhat against my better judgement, I was persuaded by visiting inspectors that in order to achieve the promotion that was ultimately my goal, and bearing in mind that I was now in my thirties, I needed to gain experience in a variety of schools. This would mean moving, preferably to an all-through primary school, and the sooner the better.

Family reasons, too, added to the pressure to move, not merely to another school, but to a less remote situation. Relying as we did on our bikes for getting around, and especially on our visits to our parents, who lived over twenty miles away, it was brought home to us that autumn that this state of affairs could not continue, - and for a very good reason; Margaret was expecting our first child.

And so, within months of the birth of our son, our house was up for sale and I had been appointed as teacher of the top-junior class in a medium-size primary school roughly midway between our native villages and our first home. Securing a house in this area presented no problem and the school lay on a regular bus route. But like so many decisions made in haste, this was one that I was soon to regret – and bitterly.

17

The danger signs were all there at the interview. The headmaster, short and bald, his florid face restless behind flashing glasses, laid great emphasis on the school's enviable record in securing grammar school places. As teacher of what he insisted in calling the scholarship class, he stressed that the successful applicant would be expected to carry on the good work. However, in response to my question, he asserted that he welcomed new initiatives of the kind that were being increasingly introduced, adding proudly that whoever was appointed could confidently expect to gain promotion to a headship within a few years, as had the two previous holders of this coveted post.

Called into the room at the conclusion of the interviews and offered the job, I sat in the chair transfixed with indecision, conscious of all eyes in the room riveted on my face. The agonising silence was interrupted by a blustery outburst from the headmaster, who clearly thought I was playing hard to get and resented the threat to his dignity. Others, he blurted huffily, would jump at the chance that I appeared to regard so lightly. I could delay my response no longer; the strain – for all concerned – was unbearable. I gulped and to my dismay heard my strangulated voice accept the offer. And I knew there and then that I had made a dreadful mistake – and a potential enemy into the bargain.

Chapter 3

I commenced my duties in the January of one of the most severe winters within living memory. To our dismay, the sale of our house had taken far longer than we had expected and this had delayed our buying of a property in the vicinity of the school. Margaret and our baby son, therefore, were living with her parents while I had obtained lodgings near the school on a Monday-to-Friday basis. The one advantage of this was that I was spared lengthy journeys to and from school, which in the prolonged freeze-up, which lasted until March, would have been difficult in the extreme. Even so, seeing my little family only at weekends, and then in cramped conditions in a grim industrial village, was at best a makeshift arrangement, one that a happy working atmosphere, such as at my previous school, would have done much to make tolerable.

Alas, I soon discovered that this was not to be. From the outset, my new headmaster let it be known that he was in the habit of spending part of every morning with my class - 'Sharpening them up', as he termed it - in preparation for the eleven-plus examination. It was made clear to me that my role was to observe this procedure, which to begin with consisted of a series of oral mental agility sessions, during which lavish praise was heaped on the brighter children while their less able classmates' faltering responses were curtly and at times contemptuously dismissed.

Worse was to follow. Mr Bacon breezed in with bundles of test papers. A stopwatch was produced and exam conditions simulated – 'To give them a feel of what the real thing will be like.' Afterwards, answers were checked, scores arrived at and problem questions analysed. I had noticed that although I had been required to submit a detailed timetable, a copy of which was displayed prominently in the classroom, Mr Bacon's lessons did not appear on it. On raising the matter, I was taken to one side and told in a conspiratorial whisper that this was because a visiting inspector could possibly interpret what went on as coaching, which was forbidden.

'It's no such thing, of course', Mr Bacon asserted, '- but you can't be too careful.' He chuckled. 'My secretary keeps an eye on the road though, just in case. She'll pop in to let me know if she spots a strange car pull up.' Sensing my uneasiness, he went on 'And if bigwig *did* walk in, we'd pretend we're teaching an English lesson. We've got to be a move ahead in this business, believe me.'

I was bemused. 'We?'

The glasses flashed challengingly. 'Yes – *we*. I'm showing you how I want it done. I'll expect you to do your share in preparing them soon.' And in case I was still in any doubt, he drove the message home. 'Your job's to get a good crop of grammar school passes, come what may. You can try out as many of your new-fangled ideas as you like once the exam's over.' He hesitated, then handed me a sheet of paper with the children's names divided into three columns.

'They're the certs,' he said, pointing to the first column. 'But drive them hard. Don't let them ease up.' The stumpy pink finger moved to the second column. 'These are the border-liners. You'll need to put a bomb under some of these. They're not natural grammar-school material but with plenty of preparation a few of them might just make it.' Again the glasses flashed their challenge. 'Once they get there, it's not our problem.'

I waited for the finger to move on to the final column - in vain. 'The rest are no-hopers,' Mr Bacon pronounced. 'Right – I'll leave you to it.'

In fact, and to my relief, the headmaster never did hand over the reins completely. As the date of the examination drew near, he spent longer than ever in my room, single-mindedly coaching the likely candidates. This he achieved by rearranging the class so that all the hopefuls were grouped together, effectively excluding the others from the 'sharpening-up' process. These children were well aware of what was happening and were only too willing to fritter away their time while their classmates were put through their paces.

And as if this flagrant violation of the rules was not bad enough, two unpleasant side-effects became increasingly evident as time passed. Mr Bacon's temper - always somewhat unpredictable - now took on the ugliness of the bully; wrong answers were ridiculed; those who hesitated were goaded into humiliation. Worse still was the effect this enforced segregation had on friendships. An 'us and them' atmosphere was created that flew in the face of all I held dear. Seething with pent-up anger, I felt powerless to intervene. All I could do, when left alone with the class, was to try to heal the divisiveness – and count the days until the dreaded exam.

March brought the long overdue thaw, and with it a buyer for our house, though not until after we had paid a hefty bill for plumbing repairs. Full of misgivings, we went ahead with the purchase of a town house, determined somehow to overcome the difficulties I had experienced in my first term; my one cause for hope being the chance of rapid promotion, as virtually guaranteed at my interview.

In an attempt to assert some kind of claim on what I was reluctant to concede had become a shared class, I invited the children to join me on a Saturday morning ramble to a prehistoric stone circle perched on a hillside not far from the school. About half the class turned up and we set off in high spirits for our destination. I had done a fair amount of background reading about the monument, including the associated folk lore, and the children listened intently as we stood before the weathered stones. Unfortunately, on the way down, one of the girls tripped and fell, spraining her ankle, and I was left with no alternative but to carry her pick-a-back fashion for the rest of the way. Far from apportioning blame, the girl's parents thanked me for bringing her safely home.

It was with a deep sense of foreboding that I knocked on Mr Bacon's office door first thing on Monday morning. I deserved, and fully expected, a reprimand for failing to inform him of my intended ramble, but nothing could have prepared me for the vicious tirade that followed. How dare I undertake such a foolhardy expedition without his consent? On no account must I repeat such a flagrant breach of his authority. It was beyond his comprehension how someone aspiring to headship could possibly behave in such a rash and irresponsible manner. I should consider myself fortunate that the accident had not been more serious. He would, of course, be writing to the girl's parents, informing them that I had been suitably admonished, etc., etc. I emerged from my superior's presence, as he no doubt intended, feeling utterly wretched, in no state to face a lively class.

The approach of Easter revealed another facet of Mr Bacon's character. I had by then become accustomed to the severe moral tone of his morning assembly addresses; now, however, the full panoply of his religious fervour was revealed, in the form of preparations for an Easter service. This event, he informed me, took precedence in the school over Christmas, which had become little more than a time of mass self – indulgence. As a Church of England lay preacher, he believed that the children should be made aware of Christ's sacrifice through active participation in their own Easter celebration, which he would as usual conduct. Again, I found myself a mere spectator as the children were rehearsed in hymns and readings on the Easter theme, the culmination of which was an interminably long and unrelentingly solemn enactment of the trial and crucifixion, with little detail spared, performed to the assembled lower classes, who sat in silent and subdued incomprehension.

However, it was during one morning midway through the summer term that my distaste for virtually all that Mr Bacon stood for finally emerged as out-and-out revulsion. True to his word, the headmaster had given me an entirely free hand once the eleven-plus was over; in fact, he had barely entered the classroom except to have a brief word with me and on these occasions ignored the children completely. On this particular morning, however, he breezed into the room, face beaming, waving aloft an envelope containing, he announced triumphantly, something we had all been waiting for – the results of the eleven-plus. He was beside himself with delight. For not only had the school maintained its second-to-none reputation for the percentage of passes to grammar school, but this year it had excelled even that record! He then went on to read out the names of those who had been successful, reserving special praise for several border-line children who, he informed us, had managed through sheer hard work to scrape through by the skin of their teeth.

That done, he turned his attention to the handful of children whom he had segregated with the other hopefuls but who had failed to secure the coveted places. True to his principles to the last, Mr Bacon did not shirk from his task. Instead, he spelt out loud and clear to this unhappy little band that they had only them-selves to blame for their failure. However, he reminded them, all was not lost; providing they applied themselves unstintingly to their work at the secondary modern school, there remained a slight yet possible chance that transfer to the grammar school could be effected at some later stage. There was even a crumb of comfort of sorts for the no-hopers; it had been known, Mr Bacon conceded, for hard-working also-rans to make good in the world; it was up to them to give of their best and put whatever modest talents they possessed to the best possible use.

Sickened by what I had just witnessed, and at a loss to know how to cope with the situation, I made discreet enquiries in the staff room. My colleagues - without exception a friendly and helpful group - were, it emerged, well aware of the iniquitous goings-on in the top junior class. Speaking in subdued voices, conscious of the presence of the headmaster in the adjoining room, they expressed surprise that I found the state of affairs disturbing; it had been assumed that like my predecessors, I was a willing party to Mr Bacon's ways. One teacher, working out his last remaining years before retirement, responded to my question about whether I should seek an appointment with the county inspector with a hollow laugh.

'You won't find much sympathy there, I'm afraid. All that would do would be to scupper your chances of promotion. Your best bet is to start applying outside the county – and the sooner the better.'

Which, after a great deal of soul-searching during the summer holiday, I decided to do. After all, I was thirty-two and had been teaching now for five years. Before that, I had had ten years' experience in industry and had two excellent testimonials from my previous schools. I decided to tackle Mr Bacon about the matter early in the new school year; I would need a testimonial from him too, whatever he chose to include in it. I suspected that he would regard this premature quest for a headship as arrogance. So be it. I had to get away, and if I failed to secure a headship, then I'd settle for another assistant post – anything other than remain where I was.

It proved to be a difficult interview. How could he be expected, Mr Bacon demanded, not unreasonably, to comment in any detail about the qualities of a teacher he had known for a mere two terms? But if I had resolved to apply for promotion elsewhere at this stage, then he would do his best to support me. I did realise, he hoped, that I was embarking on what could prove to be a long

24

and frustrating experience? I faced months of form-filling, uncertainty and disappointment. Village school headships were very much sought after and vacancies attracted scores of applicants, many of whom were highly qualified, often already deputy heads of large schools. Still, if I had made up my mind to pursue that course of action, then he would be the last person to stand in my way.

The testimonial, when it came, was supportive beyond anything I had dared to hope for. I was, I read, highly ambitious, at the peak of my powers, and in the writer's opinion, eminently suitable promotion material, etc. Did all this mean, I pondered half - ashamedly, simply that he wanted to get rid of me? My ambition, such as it was, was to get away from a regime I found detestable, that was in fact making me physically ill. That apart, it could be that I had reached the stage at which genuine fulfilment could only be attained through having my own school. And now, another factor had to be considered – Margaret was expecting our second child in the spring and a growing family would make promotion highly desirable financially.

And so I began combing the headship vacancy lists in *Teachers' World*, while at the same time immersing myself in my daily teaching, determined to live up to – and exceed – all that had been written about me.

Chapter 4

In time, the hours spent filling in headship application forms began to bear fruit. Though unsuccessful, my first two interviews – in Shropshire and Buckinghamshire – provided valuable experience so that when I was invited to attend a third - in Oxfordshire - I felt reasonably confident. Oxfordshire, I knew, had a reputation for a progressive approach to primary education and as the school in question was situated on the edge of the Cotswolds, I had every incentive to make the most of my chance.

On my two previous interviews, I had faced long and difficult journeys, one by bus, the other by train. However, on this occasion my friend and former mine surveying colleague, Walter Thorne, now the owner of a stately old Rover car, offered to take a day of his leave to drive me down, which I gratefully accepted. Meticulous as ever, Walter had planned our route in precise detail, allowing ample time for the journey. Like me, his knowledge of the Cotswolds was limited to one short holiday and the last stage of the drive, on a promise-filled April morning, was the perfect introduction to part of the region unknown to us both.

As intended, we arrived early, having eaten our sandwich-lunch on the way. The village, we discovered, lay off main roads, its two streets of mellow stone-built houses striking off from a large tree-fringed green, on the far side of which stood the school, with head teacher's house alongside. Walter parked at the opposite end and we set off on a leisurely and largely silent exploration, each absorbed in his own thoughts. The village seemed to slumber in the midday warmth; not a soul stirred, and scarcely a sound interrupted the silence. Yet this was no dormant or decaying place; a notice board outside the substantial village hall was covered with announcements of coming events. The windows of two general stores displayed a range of wares; there was an inn and a post office and surprisingly, a small discreetly-sited factory. At the far end of the main street, a lychgate gave access to a well-tended churchyard, above which rose a noble tower, fashioned, like the rest of the building, in warm, mellow stone. All in all, we agreed, this was a very pleasant place indeed. Whoever was destined to become head of its school was truly fortunate. Dare I hope that this time it would be me?

Back at the green, we could see that there was still no activity at the school so we decided to take a closer look. The buildings, in contrast to the rest of the village, looked decidedly out of place, being pebble-dashed and roofed with slate, obviously dating from the time of the first world war or thereabouts. The teacher's house alongside bore the same stamp. Outward appearance apart, the building offered plenty of space to accommodate its forty-odd children. There was an extensive playground, with what appeared to be an orchard behind, and the school overlooked open fields from its hilltop perch. Between the school house and the crossroads lay an expanse of ground, partly given over to allotments and partly what appeared to be an overgrown patch, bordering on the school orchard . A ready-made nature study area? The possibilities were exciting.

By now we could see cars arriving and men in sober suits hovering around the school, making desultory conversation with fellow interviewees. I sensed that Walter was growing increasingly ill at ease - lest, I suspected, that he too was taken for a candidate, so we agreed that he would set off on a longer walk but would be back at the car in a couple of hours. Left to myself, and having no wish to enter into small talk, I decided to take a closer look at the overgrown area behind the school, which appeared to be accessible from the gate into the allotments. Sure enough, I was able to get quite close to my objective, which I could now see had once been part of much larger allotments but had for some time been surrendered to invasive sallow, ash and hawthorn and was already

27

providing congenial habitat for several species of birds.

Together with five other candidates – all men – I was shown into a sparsely furnished little room and the long wait began. Every twenty minutes or so, the door opened and a cheerful fresh-faced man, who turned out to be the area primary adviser, invited the next interviewee to accompany him, putting each of us at ease as he led the way to the interview room.

Once inside, I was welcomed by the chairman of the school managers, an elderly distinguished gentleman, who, after effecting introductions and discharging other preliminaries, handed over to the senior primary adviser. Miss Emily Morton proceeded to demonstrate that she had given careful consideration to my application and while in sympathy with its contents, was determined to make me justify every word. In appearance not unlike a buxom farmer's wife, she was at pains to ensure that my professed belief in placing the environment at the heart of my teaching strategy was not merely an assumed ploy but something to which I was thoroughly committed and to which I had given considerable thought.

Now, for the first time, I was invited to put my case for what I stood for clearly and unequivocally. Any suspicion of woolly thinking or ambiguity was immediately seized upon and I was challenged to explain; any point emphasised which met with her wholehearted approval was rewarded with an encouraging smile. Eventually, after responding to questions from the school managers, I was thanked and asked to wait. Longing for fresh air, I made for the outer door, my mind still teeming; I had given my all. Would it be enough?

After what seemed an age, I learned - almost to my disbelief - that it was. I was called in, offered the post, accepted it with alacrity, had my hand pumped, my back slapped, commiserated briefly with fellow interviewees and after making arrangements with the correspondent to visit the school later in the term, floated, rather than walked across the green to the waiting car. Walter, dozing in the late-afternoon sunshine, awoke with a start to hear the news. We were just about to head for home when I noticed the area adviser approaching across the green. I wound down the window and introduced Walter.

'Thought I'd offer my congratulations and my wholehearted support next September,' he smiled, adding as an afterthought, 'I saw you mooching along the hedgerow behind the school. Thought then – that's a chap after my own heart!'

Walter broke the silence suddenly as we drove homeward. 'Where will you live?'

My euphoria took a nosedive back to reality. 'In the school house, I suppose. Why?'

My friend weighed his words carefully before replying. 'It's just that – well, I took a look around the outside while the interviews were on and – well, it looks a bit – primitive. Compared with where you live now, that's all.'

Nothing more was said. Instead, I found myself reviewing the afternoon's events with a perplexity bordering on panic. Our second child - a darling baby girl - had arrived to delight us ten days earlier. Could I be responsible for pitching my family into a primitive school house in unfamiliar surroundings, merely to advance my career? Conflicting thoughts jostled in my mind for the remainder of the journey home.

A letter in an unfamiliar hand arrived a couple of days later. The writer introduced himself as a Mr Henley, who, as vice-chairman of the school managers at my interview, had, I recalled, asked a question or two in a cultured voice and had congratulated me warmly at the close of the proceedings. After once more proffering congratulations, Mr Henley went on to explain his reason for writing – the question of the school house. He had, he said, been most concerned that it had been assumed that I would be taking up the

29

tenancy without having been given the opportunity to inspect the house, which was to receive a long-overdue refurbishment before I took up my appointment. He went on to say that should I, after consultation with my wife, decide to move in, he would undertake to supervise the work personally, being retired and with time on his hands, and would gladly supply such details as room and window measurements as and when required. Aware too that I did not drive, he would willingly meet me at the nearest station whenever I was able to come over before taking up my duties, and his wife would provide me with lunch.

Our relief at receiving this letter was considerable. We had resigned ourselves, with many misgivings, to exchanging our modern semi for a primitive cottage, at least for the foreseeable future. Now it seemed the change would be less of an ordeal than we had feared.

The last day of term, and of my brief spell at the school, was one of a strange mingling of emotions. My class, too, were leaving, bound for their respective secondary schools. For my part, I was leaving, not just the school but the county of my birth and which I loved – and still love – more than any other. .Mr Bacon, who since the handing-in of my notice had on the whole been pleasant enough, brought our brief leave-taking to a close with a sombre warning.

'Headship of a small school is no bed of roses, as you'll soon find out,' he reminded me. 'You'll need to watch that you don't burn yourself out.' I braced myself for a valedictory sermon but to my relief, none came. A token handshake and I was free.

Chapter 5

We moved into the school house early in August. Mr Henley had been as good as his word; he had gone to great pains to send detailed measurements of floors and windows, thus enabling carpeting and curtaining to be attended to, and the house itself, though fairly basic compared with our previous home, had been decorated inside and out and was, if not exactly modern, at least habitable.

By now, the painters had turned their attention to the school, which meant that there was little I could do by way of preparation for the coming term. A radio blared; the walls had been stripped of the displays of work I had seen at my interview; books and equipment were concealed beneath dust sheets; and the men let it be known that my presence among the paint cans and ladders was tolerated rather than welcomed.

And so, with my two-year-old son in his pushchair, I explored the village. And not just the lanes I had walked with Walter, but the bridleways and even some of the footpaths, lifting child and carriage over stiles where necessary and in so doing discovering delightful though apparently seldom-frequented walks within easy reach of our new home. In particular, I took a closer look at the overgrown area bordering the school orchard, which, providing I could obtain permission, I saw as offering rich potential for work with the children.

As luck would have it, I had chanced upon a wonderfully inspiring book shortly before our move to the Cotswolds and my evenings spent devouring it reinforced my determination to base my teaching on the local environment in the widest possible sense. In *An Experiment in Education*, Sybil Marshall described how on becoming head of a small village school, she evolved her own method of integrating the children's learning experience through art and music. Much of this experience took place out of doors, and I was especially drawn to her uninhibited way of informing any visiting inspector why her classroom was empty: 'On the cracked old American cloth covering my desk I would write large in white chalk:- 'Gone painting. Find us in the field behind the Congregational chapel.' Why shouldn't I do likewise? After all, Miss Morton had encouraged me to expand on my beliefs on how best children learn and had clearly endorsed my outlined intentions. And the area primary adviser had gone out of his way to add his own words of encouragement. So what was I waiting for? Only for the new term to begin and for the children – bright-eyed and eager to learn – to arrive.

As yet, I had seen surprisingly little of these children. Two small girls had smiled coyly from the swings on the green as I passed on my way to the post office one morning and I'd been aware of a small group of boys hanging around outside the school gate on their bikes one day as I mowed the front lawn. Were there really forty children, aged between four and ten, scattered around the village and awaiting, like me, the first day of the new school year in our freshly-painted school?

Well no, not exactly. A furtive grope under the dust sheet into the head teacher's desk drawer revealed a list of names and addresses, from which I learned that of the forty on roll, five children came from the nearby town, another four from neighbouring villages, and a further half dozen or so lived on outlying farms. I recalled that during the wait to be summoned for interview, one of the other candidates, who lived locally, had predicted that the school could well be in danger of closure in a few years through declining numbers. A tiny cloud of doubt suddenly appeared on a hitherto clear horizon.

I raised the matter with Pat Driver, the infants' teacher, who joined me in school after the painters at last departed. She produced a provisional roll, supplied by the health visitor, and together we scrutinised the figures. As we did so, I noticed that she referred to certain families as living in Baby Alley, which was not the name on the sheet. Innocently, I asked why she used what was obviously a local name. Pat, a pleasant woman a few years my senior and herself a native of the area, hesitated before replying with a blushing smile, 'Shall we say that the alley has something of a reputation for fertility?' I decided not to pursue the matter further at that stage; what concerned me most were the school's future prospects, and thanks to the mothers of Baby Alley and elsewhere, the prognosis gave me cause for hope.

In fact, it was not until some time later that I learnt how Baby Alley got its name. Apparently many years before, a childless woman who longed for motherhood, having failed to win round her reluctant husband, sought medical advice without his knowledge and was given a potion to cure her infertility. On discovering the medicine and realising its purpose, the enraged husband emptied it into the communal well, with the result that nine months later, several births occurred in the alley.

It was not until the arrival of the two playground supervisors just before midday on the first day of term that I met all my staff. By this time I had settled and registered the twenty-three juniors, collected dinner money, exchanged a few introductory words with the cook and her assistant, dealt with numerous phone calls – had in fact been on the go without a moment's let up – and yet had somehow devoted hardly any time to the most important task of all – teaching.

The two other members of the school's complement, the caretaker and the part-time teacher, I had met already. The former, a willing and conscientious woman, assisted unofficially by her husband, lived close by, while the part-time teacher I had encountered in one of her other roles, as occasional assistant in her husband's general store. We agreed that she would continue on her two-afternoons – weekly arrangement, teaching art to the juniors, thus relieving me to catch up on administrative duties.

I had just introduced myself to the two playground supervisors when Lucy and Eileen, the two fourth-year juniors who had taken it upon themselves to advise me on a range of classroom matters during the morning, approached once more.

'It's nearly twelve o'clock,' announced Lucy gravely. My failure to make the awaited connection was all too evident.

'It's time for weather,' contributed Eileen. 'We always do weather at twelve o'clock,' she added patiently.

'And we'll need new groups,' prompted Lucy. 'Some of the old group leaders have left.'

I rummaged among the sheaf of notes left by the staff supply teacher, who had been in charge during the previous term. Sure enough, weather recording was a daily and - to me - alarmingly complex activity involving all the juniors. To my shame, I had completely overlooked it in the hurly burly of the morning

The girls produced a large cardboard box. 'All the old weather records are in here,' said Lucy. 'We shall need new graphs for max and min and for rainfall. Oh, and a new chart for daily readings. The others will manage for a bit.'

'They go on the pinboard in the corridor,' Eileen informed me. 'Shall we put them up?'

I accepted the offer gratefully and asked if they'd mind taking as many of the readings as they could until I could get things organised. The girls exchanged glances. 'We'll do what we can – for now,' Lucy promised.

At the end of afternoon school, I took a deep breath and immersed myself in the weather records box. It soon became clear that my predecessor, who as I already knew had a distinct interest in mathematics and physical geography, had made weather recording an important feature of the school day. Temperature, barometric pressure, wind speed and direction, cloud type and cover – all had been dutifully recorded on charts, tables and graphs. A band of volunteers had even measured the amount of rainfall over the school holidays. I could, of course, sweep all this away in traditional new-broom style; for the first time in my working life I was free to make my own decisions – power indeed! On balance, however, it seemed wise to continue with the recording; it provided a thread of continuity to the daily routine and as long it was not allowed to degenerate into a meaningless ritual, it was a way of getting the children to work together, to promote awareness of their surroundings and to enrich their use of language.

But first of all, I had to ensure that I was familiar with all the processes. Should I attempt to achieve this on my own, or might it be a good idea to come clean about my ignorance of weather recording at the outset and seek enlightenment from those best equipped to offer it – Lucy and Eileen? This might be no bad idea, I decided. As well as an extensive range of weather recording equipment, much of it home-made, my predecessor had bequeathed among other things an improvised theodolite and tripod, a number of large-scale Ordnance Survey maps of the area and an assortment of tapes, measures and mathematical apparatus. The sobering thought struck me that with his all too obvious interest in the subject, he would have made a far greater success of surveying than I ever did. More to the point: how would I make out as his successor? Somewhat ruefully I contrasted my own position with that of Sybil Marshall, as described in *An Experiment in Education*. She had inherited a failing school and had proceeded to transform it into a thriving and successful one; I, on the other hand, was following a head who, in a different way, had made a similar impact. The missionary work, in other words, had already been done. And as though to drive the message home, one of the school managers — no doubt with the best of intentions – had made a point of congratulating me on taking over such a successful school. True enough, depending on which way you looked at it. One thing at least was crystal clear. I had been entrusted with the responsibility of building on that success by whatever means I chose. What a responsibility – and what a challenge!

Chapter 6

To say I found the going hard would be an understatement of monumental proportions. And as if never having taught lower juniors, except on school practice, was not enough, I was now responsible for a class of twenty-three children, ranging in age from seven to eleven and in ability right across the spectrum. Gone were the showpiece lessons; the sea of eager faces and clamouring responses; the chalk and talk; the stacks of identical text and exercise books. In their place I had to devise group activities and individual assignments, dividing my precious time as evenly as possible so that everyone had a fair share, and ensuring that all children progressed to the optimum of their ability in basic literacy and numeracy.

From time to time, usually at the end of the school day, I took stock of the situation. Considering that I was learning on the job, so to speak, most of the children seemed to be reasonably well motivated. There was never enough time, of course, and there were occasions when I was tempted to look back wistfully at my 'stoking' days, when my work consisted primarily of feeding the fuel into the furnace of a razor-sharp, irrepressible class of ten-year-olds. I had a few children of comparable academic ability in my present class and one of my concerns was that despite the absence of a sizable peer group, their potential should somehow be given the scope to develop across the entire curriculum.

I talked this over with the head of the neighbouring school, who like me, had arrived in the Cotswolds after teaching mainly 'A' stream classes in urban schools in the north. He confessed that after four years in his present post, the matter still exercised his mind a great deal. He'd experimented with individual and small-group assignments with varying success but there was no panacea. Generally speaking, he observed, village children learnt at a slower pace than their town and suburban contemporaries but they got there in the end:

'They won't be rushed, these Cotswold kids,' he summed up. 'They've had to adjust to me, up to a point, but like it or not, I've had to do some adjusting too, and it hasn't been easy.' Reassuring words, these – and wise ones too, I was soon to discover.

Thanks in no small part to Lucy and Eileen, I at length mastered the intricacies of the weather station and decided to invest in a school version of a Stevenson screen in which to keep the instruments. Robert and Gary, two other fourth-years whose interest had been lukewarm until called upon to help me with the assembling of the screen, now expressed intense enthusiasm for weather recording and demanded their share of responsibility for organising the weekly rota. To begin with, Lucy and Eileen were reluctant to allow what they saw as an unwarranted intrusion on their preserves; we eventually settled for a compromise the girls on duty one week, the boys the next.

The onset of autumn brought new interest to our recording. Temperatures plummeted, we noted the first frosts, and drifts of leaves descended from the ashes and sycamores close to the school. Meanwhile, the beeches and horse chestnuts fringing the green took on their rich autumnal hues and keenly-contested conker battles provided entertaining spectator- sport at playtimes. At weekends, meanwhile, I joined the scattered little groups of blackberry pickers working their way along the hedgerows and occasionally rose early enough to compete with the few hardy regulars combing the fields in search of mushrooms.

In his weekly letter (my parents had no telephone), my father, by now in his mid-eighties, declared his and my mother's intention of paying us a visit. Like us, they had no car, and as the journey from Derbyshire to the Cotswolds entailed a complicated bus-and-train link-up, I dismissed his words as wishful thinking.

How wrong this proved to be, for on Father's instructions, Mother, on her weekly shopping expedition into the nearby town, arranged for a hire car to bring them over one Saturday on a 240-mile round trip.

Neither parent had travelled further south than my uncle's farm in Leicestershire before and Father, a joiner by trade, enthused about the honey-coloured stone built villages they passed through on the journey. It so happened that a group of boys had been engaged in model-making with wood scraps in a corner of the classroom and Father, noticing the tools on the work bench, was quick to take me to task for failing to keep the saws well sharpened.

My parents' all-too-brief visit proved to be Father's last; he died suddenly a little over a year later – thankfully not before he had seen for himself how I had made amends for a failed first career.

Winter, which had flexed its muscles threateningly once or twice in the weeks leading up to Christmas, finally tightened its grip in the new year. The ground was white and hard with frost and cries of rapture echoed across the playground as the delights of sliding were rediscovered. Snow followed in the weeks ahead; a motley variety of gloves steamed on radiators, milk bottles had to be thawed out, and the caretaker patiently swept snow from doorways and spread salt on the places where slides crossed the path to the school gate.

Our daily weather recording took on a dramatic aspect - ice in the rain gauge; thermometers registering on or near the foot of their scale; plus tingling fingers, steamy windows and burst pipes. The weather affected us all. It was the natural talking point, and we talked.

We walked too. After one snowfall, we ventured out into the silent world and after staring in wonder at the way that familiar features in the local landscape had been transformed, turned our attention to animal and bird tracks. There was no doubting the children's curiosity but the experience served also to confirm my growing conviction that the often-repeated assertion that country children possessed an intimate knowledge of nature was something of a myth. It may have been true in times past, but by the 1960s, mass-media entertainment, and the dubious values it promoted, had more or less ensured that the country child's affinity with his surroundings was at most superficial.

The one exception among the older children was Anthony. I had encountered him from time to time on my wanderings, more often than not lurking with his air rifle by the river. On the occasions when he was unable to evade me, he assumed a casual air, responding to my greeting with a scarcely audible mumble, his eyes avoiding mine. Many and colourful were the tales told of him by the other children – slaughterer of bird and beast; stealer of eggs; torturer of any living thing he could lay his hands on; as well as scrumper of apples from the trees in the school orchard - an annual event which apparently took place a month or so before the fruit was edible.

A loner by temperament, reserved to the point of surliness, Anthony was the only child - apart from his similarly withdrawn younger brother Alan – to reveal any close affinity with the countryside. I tried, though with little success, to get him to communicate his knowledge to the other children. Perhaps next spring, when, as I hoped, we would obtain permission to manage the derelict allotments next to the school as a nature and conservation area, I could somehow bring about a poacher-turned- gamekeeper transformation on Anthony in the final term of his primary school life. What an achievement that would be.

The snow at length departed but winter had a few surprises still in store before finally yielding to the advance of spring. One

March morning, we became aware of a change in the weather outside. It had been a gleaming, glittery start to the day, with a fresh breeze buffeting the school on its hilltop perch. But now - suddenly, dramatically - the sky darkened and it became difficult to see the books before us. Children looked up from their work enquiringly; someone called for the lights to be switched on. Gareth, however, easily distracted at the best of times and agile as a monkey, was already at the window, craning his neck upwards.

'Cor, just look at the sky over Chippy!' he exclaimed.

I managed to head off the rush for the windows and re-direct it towards the door. As we spilled out into the playground a remarkable sight met our eyes. The patchwork of fields sloping down the shallow valley towards the local town was bathed in an intense yellow light. Every feature – barn, copse, tree, hedgerow – stood out in brilliant larger-than-life detail. While from the north-west, bearing down upon the scene with steady relentless progress, rolled a phalanx of angry smoke-grey cloud, obliterating the distant slopes in its advance. Meanwhile, over our heads, the canopy of blue-black cloud that had darkened the classroom, rolled majestically on, leaving us literally high and dry. As we watched in silent fascination, the driving rain sheet below finally engulfed the luminous panorama, causing every familiar feature to disappear from view.

'Look – look at Chippy,' someone exclaimed '- it's gone!'

'Wow – can't see a thing!'

'Watch – Boulter's Barn'll be next – look!'

'It's almost there - wait!'

'Gone – vanished. Not a sign!'

Excitement knew no bounds as we watched the storm roll on towards our neighbouring village, huddled on the opposite slope. For a moment it seemed that the wind had shifted direction sufficiently to carry the storm beyond the houses grouped around the giant church tower; but then, as we stood riveted, the entire ridge seemed to dissolve before our gaze and there was a spontaneous

41

whoop of satisfaction as finally the tower, a landmark for miles around, also disappeared. Satiated, we turned to go back indoors. 'Look – there's a rainbow!' someone exclaimed. We paused to admire its fleeting beauty, the grand finale to a spellbinding performance.

I was soon to discover that there was more to the glee that greeted the disappearance of the neighbouring village in the dramatic storm than I had at first assumed. A form of rivalry, bordering on downright dislike, had, it seemed, existed for many years and some of the children were only too willing to perpetuate it. Its origins stemmed from the fact that whereas our village, having no resident squire, prided itself on its independence, our neighbour remained firmly in the grip of the feudal tradition, complete with venerable old manor house and its titled occupant. Many were the stories told in the village concerning the various occasions in which 'we' had outsmarted 'them', not only on the sporting field but in every other imaginable situation too. One oft-repeated tale concerned an old villager who on being widowed and finding it hard to cope, had been invited to live with his daughter, who to his displeasure had married a man from the neighbouring village and had gone to live there. His response was supposedly that he would rather have been hanged in his native village than die a natural death a couple of miles up the hill.

Chapter 7

For some time I had cast a covetous eye on the derelict allotments bordering the school playground. They had attracted my attention on the day of my interview and I decided that the time had come to find out if we could put them to use as a conservation study area. The parish council, understandably enough, was cautious. We were free to make use of the overgrown and long-since abandoned area at the far end of the allotments but if we wished to extend our activities to include the more recently vacated plots adjacent to the school, then we would have to pay the annual rate for each – six shillings. I did a quick calculation; together, the rent-free overgrown area – the most valuable for our purposes – plus the six plots nearest the school, covered about an acre; it couldn't be better – and all for less than two pounds a year!

We took possession of our newly-acquired estate early in the new term. First the juniors, then the infants, filed along the path, noticing the emerging celandines at our feet amid the lush green mantle of early spring. Once the juniors reached the abandoned area, however, the path was virtually obliterated. We faced a miniature forest of palm-bearing sallows, ash saplings, hawthorn scrub and bramble patches, which was instantly likened to jungle, through which we - an intrepid band of fearless explorers - had to force our way, watched from a safe distance by the overawed infants.

I noted with satisfaction that natural regeneration had reached such an advanced stage that some of the ashes and the odd sycamore were up to fifteen feet high, while the clumps of hawthorn and bramble were already sufficiently impenetrable as to offer secure nesting sites for birds.

Soon afterwards, I had a visit from one of the county's rural studies advisers, who was to become a valuable ally in my plans to place environmental studies at the heart of the school's curriculum. He not only recognised the potential value of a nature study and conservation area but readily agreed to help with funding for tree-planting and site management generally as and when needed. In the meantime, a farmer member of the school managers donated a number of spruce and larch trees which, though not exactly my preferred choice, nevertheless gave the children their first opportunity to try their hand at planting and in time provided a useful screen for a length of unsightly metal fencing along the edge of the school playground.

As yet I had made little headway in my bid to win round Anthony to the conservation cause. Like his peers, he seemed to take an interest in our outdoor studies but still displayed a marked unwillingness to communicate his knowledge or to do more than the absolute minimum of follow-up work in the classroom .Then one afternoon, during a discussion on the diet of foxes - Kay Elton having just related how a fox had wrought havoc in her father's poultry house – Anthony spoke out.

'Oi knows where there's a dead fox', he blurted. 'Oi can bring yo its skellin'on if yo loikes.'

I jumped at the offer. Could this be the long-awaited breakthrough? At least, it was a step in the right direction. Sure enough, next morning Anthony appeared with a large plastic fertiliser sack, which he dumped unceremoniously by my desk.

''ere's that skellin'on what yo wanted,' he declared in bolder-than-usual tones. 'Our dad wants th' sack back, though.'

A gasp of disgust broke from some of the girls. 'Oi've seen it – it's 'orrible!' one exclaimed.

I took a tentative peep. I knew instantly what she meant. Far from having reached the skeleton stage, the fox was merely in an advanced state of putrefaction. The stench was appalling. I grasped the bag and made for the door. 'Thanks very much, Anthony,' I managed through gritted teeth. 'We'll – I'll - bury it for now and we'll dig it up when it's – ready.'

After school, accompanied by Anthony, anxious to retrieve his sack, I hurriedly interred the corpse near the entrance to the nature area .Anthony was at pains to mark the spot with a stick. 'Should get a real good skellin'on outa that afore oi leave,' he remarked. 'Oi knows where there's a badger an' a rabbit an' all. Let me know when yo wants 'em.'

'I will, Anthony, I will,' I promised. '- and do thank your father for lending the sack.'

We turned our attention to moles. Prompted no doubt by Anthony's contribution, a younger boy brought in a recently expired mole and we spent some time examining it and discussing the ways in which it was adapted to its unusual mode of life. Someone remarked that there were several molehills in the school orchard and we decided to investigate. I had already told the children something of what life was like for humans working underground and wonder was expressed that such a tiny creature could excavate such a vast amount of earth in its search for worms. Wild guesses were made as to the weight of the molehills so, eager to capitalise on this interest, I dispatched volunteers to fetch scales and weights and soon the weighing process was in full swing.

We were so absorbed in our task that it was not until an unfamiliar voice joined in the discussion that I realised that we had a visitor - none other than one of Her Majesty's Inspector of Schools. Tall and impeccably dressed, he extended a hand to shake the one I was hurriedly wiping before joining in the activity, or rather questioning the children on the whys and wherefores of what they were doing.

At length, having attracted a sizable group into his orbit, he judged the time was ripe to lighten the mood by posing a well-worn rhetorical question: 'Does anyone know how to distinguish molehills thrown up by males from those of females?' Needless to say, the question, delivered in avuncular tones with a wink in my direction, was met with absolute silence. 'Simple', H.M.I. declared, clearly relishing the anticipation of what was to follow. 'Male moles know exactly where they're going, so they tunnel in a straight line, throwing up their hills likewise.' Knowing what came next, I awaited the reaction with interest, as the inspector went blithely on to assert that female moles, lacking a similar sense of direction, drove their tunnels in haphazard fashion, scattering their hills at random in the process.

I knew enough about the quick reactions of one or two of the brighter girls to feel sure that this misogynistic witticism would not go unchallenged. And I was not to be disappointed. Jacqueline - for ever alert to any remark remotely disparaging towards her sex, and something of an actress into the bargain - gave vent to a loud and theatrically hollow laugh.

'Ha, ha – *very* funny!' Lesson learned, H.M.I. turned his attention to me, seemed satisfied with my responses, and was soon on his way.

We returned to school after the Easter holiday towards the end of April. The nine fourth-year children were beginning their final term in the primary school before transferring to the local comprehensive in September. During the weeks ahead they were to meet their new headmaster, who liked to visit all the schools in his catchment area for an informal chat with future pupils, to be followed by a visit with their parents to their new school during the final week of term. I was pleased to learn that they would be entering mixed-ability classes, where hopefully their talents would be recognised and their potential attained.

The high-spiritedness which became increasingly evident as the term progressed was natural enough, as were the first signs of interest in the opposite sex, expressed in bizarre and at times uncharacteristic behaviour. I found it difficult to envisage the school without these children; as the newcomer, I had relied on them in many ways and had seldom found them wanting. Lucy and Eileen, especially, had proved almost indispensable during my first term and had obviously thrived on the responsibility. Robert and Gary too, had emerged; as the 'strong men' of the school, they had shone in any situation demanding practical expertise. Following their successful assembling of the Stevenson screen, they had repaired the infants' Wendy house; fitted new handles to the caretaker's brooms; and given up their own time to repairing the sandpit wall in the playground. They had in fact tackled any task with relish and were at their happiest on their knees with hammer and nails, surrounded by a crowd of admiring younger children.

Even Anthony's last weeks had been comparatively rewarding. I had finally succumbed to his pleas to exhume the fox, which to my relief had by now been reduced to a virtual skeleton and we had been able to clean, assemble and label the bones on a plasticine base for display at the parents' evening.

Late one afternoon towards the end of term, I had another visit from Bill, the area primary adviser, who had called several times during my first year. We stood talking at the school gate; the children had gone home and we paused to watch the house martins weaving their intricate patterns in the air above us before streaking like arrows to their nests under the eaves of the school roof. I had been lamenting how the speeding days left insufficient time to achieve all I had set out to do. After patiently hearing me out, Bill went to great pains to reassure me that I had made a good start. Gesturing with a sweep of the arm to include the school, the surrounding fields, the village and the tireless martins above, he reminded me of the enthusiasm with which I had made my case at my interview.

'What more could you want – children and countryside? Enjoy them both – together. That way, you're bound to succeed.' There was a warm twinkle in his eye and no mistaking the conviction in his voice.

Chapter 8

Choosing a suitable book to share with a class of such varied age and ability proved to be far from easy. I settled eventually for Meindert Dejong's *The Wheel on the School*, the story of how the pupils of a Dutch village school erected a wheel on the roof to attract storks to breed. It proved to be a popular choice, for birds were beginning to play an important part in the everyday life of the school. Our house martins were still rearing their last broods and our bird table would soon be providing a valuable catering service for the resident birds as winter approached.

Teacup in hand, I was on playground duty one morning when Tom Elton's Land Rover drew up outside the school gate. 'Kay tells me you want an old wheel,' he called. 'Will this do?' I must have looked somewhat mystified. 'Something about a book you've been reading to them,' he added helpfully. 'Anyway, come and have a look at it.'

In the back of the Land Rover lay a giant cartwheel, its huge hub and splayed wooden spokes still bearing traces of red paint. It had, Tom informed me, once belonged to a traditional Oxfordshire wagon. He laughed when I explained Kay's misunderstanding. 'Thought it sounded a bit odd. Wondered if you'd got carried away explaining about the birds and the bees!'
I had no hesitation in accepting the gift however, and we unloaded and manoeuvred it carefully across the playground, watched by a throng of wondering children. I mentioned that I would probably get Sid Hopkins, the caretaker's husband, to assist me to install it in the corridor after giving it a lick of paint.
'He'll be in his element, will Sid,' Tom commented. 'He was apprenticed to a wheelwright – it'll be like old times to him.'

Sure enough, Sid's face - usually expressionless, in keeping with a seemingly dour personality - lit up at the sight of the wheel.

He needed no persuasion to embark on a detailed account of how it was made.

''Tis a right beauty!' he beamed. 'There's four sections to th' rim,' he said, pointing. 'T'was the devil of a job gettin' the iron tyre on – had to be done while it were still 'ot, then dipped straight into a cold trough. So that the wood expanded, see?' He stroked his chin reflectively. 'T'was an interestin' trade to learn – no call for it now, though.'

Try as I would, I could not persuade Sid to talk about wheelwrighting to the class; he did however, agree to explain to Roger and Tim - the two older boys I intended succeeding Robert and Gary - something of the craft one day after school. The pair jumped at the chance and gave a vivid account of what they had learned to the other children on the following day.

A few days later, the wheel - painted by Roger and Tim in the nearest we could get to its original colour - was proudly displayed in the corridor, where it was drawn, measured and written about in every conceivable way. Soon, interest in wheels resulted in others - ranging from pram wheels to a steering wheel and a primitive flanged wheel - being brought in. But when Maisie Howe announced that her father intended contributing an aeroplane wheel for our display, I didn't pay much attention; Maisie often made extravagant claims, which usually proved groundless. To my amazement, however, I arrived at school the following morning to discover a huge aeroplane wheel chained to a drainpipe, soon to be surrounded by gaping children. Like the Eltons, the Howes were farmers and apparently a good-natured rivalry had existed between the families for years. I didn't exactly hear Maisie say 'My wheel's bigger than yours!' to Kay Elton but the triumphant smile she flashed around the class that morning spoke eloquently enough.

Later that week, as Pat and I surveyed the collection, with its labels and associated work neatly displayed, we agreed that it should not be left to gather dust for too long. The children's interest, naturally enough, would soon wane. As we reached the doorway, where Maisie's wheel stood in splendid isolation, Pat remarked, 'If she gets a prize for the biggest, you'd better reserve another prize for me. I'm bringing my husband's old watch along tomorrow. We're going to take it to bits and hopefully find the smallest wheel so far.'

November proved to be exceptionally wet. Bonfire Night was a virtual washout and the meadows by the brook were transformed into a lake. Eventually however, strong winds took over and the drying-up process got under way .Now, wind speed readings replaced rainfall as the most coveted activity at our weather station. Arriving at school one morning, Philip caused a minor sensation by reporting that he had just seen a stork feeding on the receding flood water by the old railway crossing. Memories of *The Wheel on the School* were instantly rekindled. I suggested that the bird was most likely a heron; even so, it would be worth the short walk down to the floods in the hope of seeing such a fine bird at close quarters.

To our disappointment, the floodwater proved to be deserted. I consoled Philip, who had been subjected to some mild ridicule from a few of the older boys over what they considered to be an hilarious case of mistaken identity ('Ole Phil can't tell a stork from butter', etc.) – and then we leaned over the parapet of the bridge and discussed the role played by brooks such as ours in the draining of floodwater and the feeding of our local River Evenlode, itself a tributary of the Thames.

The interest in rivers and drainage generally that arose from our unsuccessful attempt to see a heron provided a perfect stimulus to the project on maps on which we had recently embarked. Thanks to my predecessor, we had a wide range of maps to draw upon. The large-scale sheets, in particular, provided a wealth of discussion and led to much worthwhile written work. Many of these were badly in need of revision and our attempt to bring them up to date proved to be a popular and instructive exercise. In fact, it became a kind of game, in which the children vied with one another in trying to spot omissions and discovering features no longer in existence:

'Look – there's the council houses.'

'They don't look like that now, though – it doesn't show the crescent.'

'It must have been built later.'

'What's that little building near the church?'

''Don't know - there's only graves there now.'

'My gramp says that the old school was in the churchyard when he was a boy. He says they pulled it down – it wasn't safe.'

By now, we were beginning to use maps rather like books, turning to them as a matter of course. Increasingly, they were dipped into, discussed, browsed over. They became a natural part of our way of life — taken for granted, yet treated with respect. Towards Christmas, after the floods had finally receded, it was agreed that we would spend an afternoon attempting to trace the course of the brook on the final stage of its journey to join the Evenlode. Donning our wellingtons, we set off down the hill and after viewing the brook once more from the bridge, we crossed a nearby stile and took a footpath which according to our map, followed the brook's winding course over several fields.

With one exception, none of the children had walked this way previously. Only Alan - the withdrawn and generally uncommunicative younger brother of my former pupil Anthony - confessed with some reluctance to having been this way before. So much, I reflected, for the oft-repeated myth that village children knew every nook and cranny of their locality.

Eventually, our footpath crossed the brook by a footbridge and climbed over the old railway embankment and out of the valley. I explained that as we had no permission to proceed further over private land, whose owner was unknown to me, we would have to retrace our steps. However, in response to the groans of disappointment that this announcement provoked, I decided that we would explore a stretch of the embankment, from which we could get a view of the brook as it shuffled beneath the alders towards its destination.

The branch line, which had closed only three years earlier, was fast being reclaimed by nature .Unlike me, some of the older children had seen trains travelling along the track; one girl's father had been the local signalman. Our conversation turned from brooks and rivers to railways.

Suddenly I realised that we would need to step out briskly to reach school in time for the bus to the remote hamlets. As we started back, Philip, who had been in earnest conversation with Alan, approached me. 'Alan says he knows a short cut,' he announced. Puzzled, I asked Alan to explain. 'There's a secret passage – on'y me an' our Ant'ny knows 'bout it,' he mumbled, as the other children crowded round.

Much as I welcomed this rare emergence from Alan's customary silence, I tried to explain that although I couldn't take a chance on this mysterious route today, he could show it to us on a future occasion. Alan, however, was not to be deflected so easily.

''Tis quicker than goin' back th' way we come,' he asserted. I repeated that, grateful though I was for the suggestion, I felt I couldn't take it up now. Alan looked sullen and confused and again mumbled something to Philip, who once more took on the role of intermediary. 'Alan says - can I go with him now and see who gets to the bridge first – just to prove it?' A snap decision was called for. Against my better judgement, but anxious to give Alan any encouragement I possibly could, I agreed to the request, having first extracted a solemn promise that the boys would wait by the bridge. Alan needed no further bidding; with Philip at his heels, he was off.

'And no running!' the others called after them

'No runnin'!' Alan threw back over his shoulder.

Although the rest of us stepped out at a brisk pace, as we rounded the last bend in the path we could see two figures waving triumphantly from the bridge.

'It's them – they've beaten us!'

'I bet they ran all the way.'

'It's not fair – they must have cheated!'

There was no mistaking the look of satisfaction on Alan's face as we drew near, while Philip's excitement knew no bounds. 'It was great – a real secret passage!' he burst out. '– and we're the only ones who know about it, aren't we, Alan?'

' 'Cept our Ant'ny,' Alan corrected him.

The following weekend, exercising my dog, I solved the mystery. When the bridge had been built, a low tunnel, some three feet high, had been constructed nearby to allow flood water to drain away from the road. The boys had cut across a cart track to emerge near the bridge, through the tunnel, which in dry weather was easily passable for a child. I kept my discovery to myself, to be let into the secret later with the other children. Alan went on to reveal some 'secret carving' on the bridge, which proved to be an Ordnance Survey bench mark - tying in appropriately with our work on maps.

But it was the 'secret tunnel' that appealed most to the children's imagination.

'I reckon that we ought to call it Alan's Tunnel,' Philip declared. Everyone agreed. And so - to us at least - Alan's Tunnel it became.

Chapter 9

The afternoon that a blushing Pat Driver broke the news of her pregnancy, my congratulations, though sincere enough, were tempered by the knowledge that her forthcoming departure would make a major impact on our little school. Pat made it clear that she would be leaving for good at the end of the school year as she intended devoting herself to full-time motherhood. This meant that a new, permanent infants teacher would need to be appointed and the sooner the better.

Just how fortunate I had been in having Pat as a colleague was brought home to me when the three applicants for the forthcoming vacancy were called for interview. Not one displayed the sparkle I had come to take for granted. The school managers were left with no alternative but to re-advertise. In the meantime, a temporary teacher was sought for. Yet again, the post proved difficult to fill. In the end, my part-time teacher agreed reluctantly to teach the juniors in the mornings for a term, while I taught the infants, thus enabling an experienced infants teacher, who was available only in a temporary part-time capacity, to relieve me for the afternoon session. This far from satisfactory arrangement meant that apart from the unsettling effect generally, I would lose my precious twice-weekly non-teaching afternoons.

Any previous demands on my teaching skills were as nothing compared with those I was now called upon to cope with as a teacher of a class comprised of twenty children aged from four to seven. True, my training had given me an insight into the theory of infant method, and I had two young children of my own. But nothing could have prepared me for the unrelenting demands of these young children, some of whom were in their first term at school.

Without the help of the wife of the head of the neighbouring school, not herself a teacher but pressed into service as a welfare assistant, I should never have coped. As it was, by lunchtime I was utterly exhausted and for the first time in my teaching career, faced the afternoon session with the juniors with grim determination rather than keen anticipation.

Never was my inexperience of teaching very young children more exposed than on the morning when a group were engaged in cutting out paper shapes. Unable to find sufficient pairs of scissors, I senr round to the junior classroom for more pairs and distributed them among the children. Some time later, as I was absorbed in helping one particular child, the welfare assistant sidled up to me and whispered
'I think Debbie Parslow's been cutting her hair.'
Sure enough, we discovered that Debbie, a solemn withdrawn child, had managed to hack off one of her golden tresses and that a couple of her classmates had attempted with varying success to do the same. It was not until then that I found to my cost that the borrowed scissors, unlike those used by the infants, were pointed – a lesson never to be forgotten, especially after having to apologise for the state of their daughters' hair to a trio of frowning mothers.

One autumn afternoon, just before playtime, the peace in the junior classroom was broken by the sound of horses' hooves on the road outside. Later, as I watched the juniors at play, there was no sign of the infants, and even more puzzling, a peep in their classroom revealed that it too was empty. Hearing the clatter of hooves still coming from the direction of the village green, I stepped outside the school gate, to discover the infants, with their teacher, huddled on the green, encircled by the horses of the local hunt. I learned later that my temporary colleague was a passionate champion of hunting and assumed that I, too, approved of the activity. She seemed surprised when I expressed my amazement that apart from exposing the children to risk in this way I found it incomprehensible that so many people had nothing better to do on a working day than gallop around in pursuit of foxes.

This proved to be one of many issues on which my colleague and I failed to agree. The most worrying concerned relationships with parents. While I endeavoured to treat all parents in the same way, she adopted a form of sliding scale in her dealings with mothers. This ranged from a fawning concern reserved for the affluent and articulate down to an offhand, take-it-or-leave-it attitude to those she considered her social inferiors.

It so happened that one of the mothers my colleague considered worthy of special treatment was the wife of an airline pilot. One afternoon, after the two women had chatted animatedly after school, I was informed that we were to be presented with a pair of Senegalese parakeets, which were to be installed in a purpose-built cage in the infants' classroom. My cool response met with instant indignation. Surely, as a bird lover, I was told, I should welcome this generous gesture. What possible reason could there be for denying the children the pleasure they would undoubtedly get from watching the birds' behaviour? Sure enough, the parakeets, complete with huge unsightly cage, arrived a few days later. However, my misgivings were soon confirmed by the school medical officer, who promptly decreed that the possibility of the birds carrying pssitacosis constituted a health hazard and that they should be removed immediately. It emerged later that the donors, wanting to be rid of the birds, had decided to try to off-load them on the school and had found the teacher an all-too-willing victim.

Thankfully, a stressful and demanding term offered one bright prospect for the future. A new permanent infants teacher was appointed to commence duty in the new year.

In conversation with one of the school managers, I was told that the elderly titled lady owner of a nearby estate, herself a nature lover, would willingly allow me to visit the extensive lake in the grounds to see its abundant bird life.

'She's an odd old bird, herself,' he confided. 'Deaf as a post, too. But I've put in a good word for you. I suggest you get over there fairly soon. Her memory's non too clever nowadays.'
I thanked him and promised to take advantage of the offer as soon as I possibly could.

A few days later, cycling along the winding beech-fringed drive towards the vast imposing house, the sound of gunshots close by gave rise to a feeling of uneasiness, which the towering façade of the building did nothing to dispel. Avoiding the steps to the main doorway, I headed along a fork in the drive leading towards the rear of the building and was relieved to see an open side door, near to which was parked a tradesman's van.

I was about to ring the bell when an elderly man in overalls staggered outside, carrying a bulky toolbox. 'The whole place needs re-wiring,' he grumbled, depositing his burden back in the van. 'Tried to tell 'er ladyship time an' time again. Yet will she listen? Will she 'eck?' He slammed the van door. 'Either can't hear – or won't,' he continued, climbing into the cab. 'Tried writin' it down – made no difference. Thinks I've nothin' better ta' do than be at 'er beck an' call.' He started the engine. 'Best o' luck, mate,' he called as he drove off.

I hesitated before the open door, uncertain whether or not to ring the bell. Eventually, after doing so and waiting in vain for a response, I was about to give up and depart when approaching footsteps made me wheel round. Before me stood a tall, youngish woman, clad in woolly sweater and jodhpurs, her pink cheeks surmounted by a man's flat cap, a shotgun under her arm.
'Bin shootin' bloody squirrels,' she announced by way of introduction. 'It's no use ringin' that,' she indicated the door bell. 'Mother'll never hear you.'
I explained the reason for my visit.

'First I've heard of it,' came the response,' 'Anyway, you'd better come in.' I followed her through a large and gloomy kitchen, along a corridor and into a panelled, heavily-furnished room in which sat a tiny elderly lady, a slumbering tabby on her knee.

'Fella here says you've given him permission to see the lake,' the daughter announced in a piercing screech. 'Somethin' about the birds.'

The old lady looked up, scrutinising my face keenly.
'Birds, eh?'

I attempted to jog her memory, emphasising that I merely wanted her consent to bird-watch by the lake. However, it soon became evident that I wasn't getting through to her and her daughter's attempts to put my case were faring little better.

'Tell him he's allowed to take only one egg,' the old lady instructed, her own voice only marginally less strident than her daughter's. 'One egg only, tell him – no more!'

My insistence that on no account would I interfere with nests fell literally on deaf ears. In the end I gave up, thanked her ladyship for seeing me and took my leave. The daughter, still with her shotgun under her arm, accompanied me to the door. Having established that I wasn't a shooting man, she gave a parting shrug. 'Pity. The bloody squirrels are everywhere. It'll soon be a full-time job keepin''em down.'

I never did get around to visiting the lake, though occasionally when cycling in the vicinity of the estate, I could hear the crack of a gunshot as, I assumed, another hapless squirrel fell prey to her ladyship's gun-toting daughter.

Chapter 10

'Grandpa found this by the roadside near Stow yesterday. It's alive - but only just.' Maisie Howe placed the large cardboard box on my desk one cold winter morning and awaited my response. The other children hovered around in anticipation. Maisie, typically, was determined to extract every ounce of drama from the situation. 'I don't *think* it'll peck you – it might, though.'

By now I was used to receiving such offerings. Quite undeservedly, possibly through having successfully reared a young jackdaw brought to me some time before, I seemed to have gained a reputation for rehabilitating sick wild creatures. Trust Maisie to bring the latest find in the largest box she could lay her hands on. Tentatively, I proceeded to open it.

Inside, eyes closed, its talons gripping a log of wood, was a tawny owl. Apart from its emaciated state, I could detect no trace of injury. The day was only just beginning. I had a class to teach. After allowing everyone a quick peep, I decided to put the owl, still on its perch in the box, in my office, together with water and some meat scraps from the canteen, at the same time closing the curtains to subdue the bright morning light. I then resolved to banish our feathered guest from my mind until playtime.

But I had not allowed for the children's reactions. Scarcely a few minutes passed, it seemed, without someone expressing concern for the welfare of Oliver, as the owl had been named.
'I bet he's lonely – on his own in the office.'
'What if the phone rings? It'll frighten him.'
'Course it won't. Owls don't mind noise. They make it - hooting.'
'Do you think he'll have eaten his breakfast yet?'
'Dunno. But what about when he wants to go to the toilet?'
'Owls are like hens, stupid! They just go, that's all.'
The last observation proved all too correct. Peeping round

the door at playtime, I could see that although the meat remained untouched, Oliver had managed to relieve himself over my desk, without apparently moving from his perch. At the end of the afternoon, with the owl still having scarcely touched the meat, extravagant promises were made of rats, mice and other owl-friendly morsels on the following day. In the meantime, however, I felt that a little research into owl-diet was called for. I knew from past experience that owls in the wild regurgitated bones and fur from their prey in the form of pellets, but how did one go about feeding a captive owl if the rodents promised failed to materialise? Fortunately, a book in the school library came to the rescue. In the absence of natural food, it suggested, it was worth trying to simulate this by wrapping small pieces of raw meat in chicken feathers, thus providing the necessary roughage. I phoned Maisie Howe's father.

Next morning, before school opened, Maisie and a couple of friends arrived, bearing a bag of feathers from their poultry shed. Soon we had an assembly line in action that in time produced a handful of what we hoped would be acceptable substitute prey for Oliver. It was as well that we did, for despite all the assurances that traps had been set and that cats had been instructed to bring in their nocturnal hunting spoils to help feed a hungry owl, no one was able to provide us with any natural food.

For a couple of days, our efforts seemed in vain. Still perched on his log, Oliver steadfastly refused to sample our offerings and I was inwardly reconciled to having to break the news of his death to the children when one morning Maisie, whose devotion to the bird had become all-consuming, noticed that he had left his perch and that some of the meat had been eaten. Then, to our delight, we discovered his first pellet. From then on, recovery was rapid. Fortunately, the weather had by now turned milder and a few days later, after he had been drawn, photographed and much admired, a little group of devotees gathered in the nature area at dusk to witness Oliver's return to the wild. Or at least, that what we intended. For some time, however, the owl, perched motionless on my wrist, showed no inclination whatever to gain his liberty. Unmoved by the children's pleas to take his leave, he waited until the little crowd had dwindled to a mere handful and then, without warning, he opened his wings and floated away silently between the trees into the gloom, leaving Maisie and her friends tearful and their head teacher surprised to find himself in the grip of conflicting emotions.

The Oliver episode led us to an investigation into the lives of our nearest owl neighbours. As the year advanced, the plaintive yelping call of little owls could be heard at dusk and eventually I tracked their whereabouts to the orchard behind the Eltons' farmhouse. Walking through the orchard with Tom, I was convinced that the owls were making use of a decapitated elm on the edge of the orchard and suggested that its hollowed-out upper trunk might contain evidence - in the form of pellets - of their occupation. I knew from previous conversation that Tom remained to be convinced that this alien owl was entirely innocent of preying on his poultry and game and suggested that the analysis of pellets, as carried out by the children on my final school practice, might prove interesting. Tom agreed readily enough so one day after school, equipped with a ladder, I led the way into the orchard, followed by a small group of volunteers.

Watched by her father and the rest of us, Kay Elton scaled the ladder and peered cautiously into the dark cavity. 'Can't see a thing', she called down. 'it's all rotten wood and leaves. It needs somebody small enough to get inside.' This was the perfect cue for Alan, who since the exploration of the tunnel, had emerged from his shell to an extent I had hardly believed possible. Having first satisfied myself that there was no danger involved, I gave the go-ahead and in no time the slight and agile figure had disappeared inside the rotting trunk, to emerge soon afterwards with a shout of triumph.

'Cor, there's tons o' 'em! Oi'll need a bag or some'in to put 'em in,' he called. There were in fact more than enough pellets for every child in the class to have one to dissect later. I promised Tom that we'd let him know our findings in due course.

'First it's wheels, then owls! Wonder what you'll come up with next?' my farmer friend mused. 'School's not what it was in my day, that's for sure.'

We didn't pursue the subject at the time but reflecting on Tom's words later, it occurred to me that the children's education must seem something of a mystery to many other villagers. Regular parents' evenings were held, of course, but these tended to be seen merely as routine interviews with teachers and inspection of written and number work. Perhaps the time had come to open up our activities to a wider world.

Apart from the initial reaction of a few of the younger girls, there was no sign of squeamishness as we began the painstaking task of dissecting the pellets. After all, the children were no strangers by now to the various components of the mammalian skeleton, having examined that of the fox brought in by Alan's brother Anthony in the previous year, as well as seeing other miscellaneous skulls and bones that had come from other sources since. Soon, tweezers were busily teasing out evidence of the little owls' diet as the pellets gave up their secrets.

'Look – I've found a skull – with lots o' teeth an 'all.'

'Hey, here's half of a lower jaw. Has anybody found the other half ?'

'This bone's just like that fox's, only smaller – a teeny, weeny pelvic girdle!'

'I've found some little teeth – really little. Pass me that magnifying glass quick!'

Fur comprised the chief item in most of the pellets, with shiny blue-black fragments of beetle wing-cases also common; incontrovertible proof, we concluded, that Tom Elton's little owls were innocent of crimes against his chickens and game. Insects apart, it seemed that mice and voles comprised most of the owls' diet. The next stage was for me to bleach the bones in hydrogen peroxide, after which they were carefully mounted on black card before being labelled. Coloured pictures of little owls, drawings and written accounts of our findings completed the project, ready for display at the forthcoming parents' evening.

This, I reasoned, together with the projects we had completed on rivers and maps, would demonstrate to some degree that our time spent out of doors was not only worthwhile in itself in promoting a spirit of enquiry but gave rise to a high standard of written, number, science and art work. And this, I fully intended, was only the beginning.

Chapter 11

As yet, apart from taking the occasional walk around its margins, we had made little use of our nature study and conservation area. With the arrival of spring, however, this was about to change. Jean, the new infants teacher and I agreed that from now on, all the children would experience at first hand the greening of the countryside through regular visits to our own nature reserve, as we decided it would in future be called.

Broadly speaking, our main aims would be twofold: to foster a sense of wonder, and through it, love for the natural world; and to promote a spirit of enquiry into that world. At a practical level, these aims would be realised .in a variety of ways. To begin with, we decided to concentrate on the naming of common wild plants, familiarising the children with these as they came into bloom and noting their changing form as the year advanced and fruiting succeeded flowering. Trees, insects, mammals and birds too, would be included in our studies, once again not merely as objects to name but to be observed in relation to their adaptation to their natural habitats. From this approach, we reasoned, would stem a wider understanding of the world in which we lived – a world whose wonders in all their diversity would provide the impetus for much of our work with the children across the curriculum.

As a first step towards implementing these aims, the juniors set about making a large plan of the nature reserve. Once the scale had been determined, measuring and drawing the rectangular outline was straightforward enough. Fixing the positions of prominent trees, bramble patches and other distinctive features proved something of a challenge, however, and one that the more mathematically able older children clearly relished. I had explained grid references to these children on our work on maps earlier and here was an opportunity to put theory into practice, albeit on a different scale.

Apart from the wide access track extending the entire length of the allotments, which formed its northern boundary, our nature reserve had as yet no clearly-defined paths and establishing these became one of our priorities. But where, and how many? There was much lively debate on this and eventually it was resolved that we would create a main path leading from the entrance to the reserve along the western boundary to join the allotment track and that there would be three other paths providing access to the three distinct areas of the reserve – the Forest Path, leading to the area containing the well-established clumps of hawthorn, ash and sycamore; the Jungle Path, skirting the patches of bramble; and the Rosebay Path, looping round the poorly-drained eastern extremity, so called because clumps of willow herb comprised the dominant vegetation. Names were also given to various prominent features within each area.

Naming the main path proved the most contentious of all. So many ideas were forthcoming that I decided to settle the issue with a ballot, the winner of which was Linda, who gave as her reason for suggesting Steadfast Path: 'It's already worn by our feet. It's always clear. You can rely on it being there.'

Now we could get down to tree planting in earnest. With the help of the rural studies adviser, we obtained a varied selection of indigenous trees and shrubs and planted them according to a predetermined pattern, involving children of all ages throughout. The older children made and painted wooden name-plates and commenced a written record of the planting dates and growth rates of our collection. It was gratifying to find others – school managers, parents and villagers – taking an interest in our project, to the extent of donating specimens. Tact was needed when some of these offerings proved to be garden exotics – 'to give a bit of variety and colour.' These were planted in a corner of the reserve to avoid hurting feelings. Much more welcome was a wagon-load of decaying logs - or to be more precise, sections of tree trunks - given to us by the owner of a local sawmill, which would provide excellent cover for small creatures and in time become hosts for fungi.

Our next priority was to construct a pond and bog garden, both of which we stocked with appropriate native water-loving plants. In addition, we were given a number of old sinks by a builder-parent and these were installed nearby to serve for the closer study of aquatic life.

Our one disappointment was that none of our hurriedly-made tit boxes affixed to the young trees by the Forest Path was occupied, despite reports of inspection by prospective tenants. We decided that certain modifications in design were needed and vowed to have the improved boxes ready in plenty of time for the following spring.

That summer, our nature reserve proved to be a rich source of inspiration for creative work, based on first-hand observation. We spent many afternoons working in small groups, learning to employ all our senses, confining ourselves to limited areas of the reserve, and recording our impressions in whatever ways seemed appropriate. Poetry, in particular, proved to be a favourite medium:
Thistle Den is so mysterious
Standing on its own
Infested with small creatures
Quiet and alone.

Bramble Island is surrounded
The ground beneath it makes it thrive
The wind sails through its leafy branches
Cool sprays of rain help it survive.

Our nature reserve is dense and windy
With rosebay growing thick and tall
 They seem to curl around you
When you walk through, not scared at all.

Other poets chose to express themselves in free verse:-

The Larch
The larch with its needles
So soft and so green
It sways in the wind
So gracefully and gently.

The trunk holds fast the branches
As they rock to and fro in the wind
They smell so sweet in the soft refreshing rain
And look so free as they gently sway.

Wild roses
They grow beside the Jungle Path
Which winds along the creepers
They grow tall above the soil and shrubs
Surrounded by nettles and grasses
With stamens so small and yellow
And petals like smoothest silk,
They feel like the softest feather
On a small bird's wing.

As summer advanced, the grasses by the Steadfast Path attained the height of the tallest children. There was no need now to bend or squat to examine the plants and animals in detail. Instead, they could be studied at eye level. And this we proceeded to do. The resulting artwork, depicting flower heads, ladybirds, caterpillars and other tiny creatures, revealed how keenly this teeming life had been observed and painstakingly recorded. By degrees, the nature reserve was becoming an extension of our classroom - a valuable resource for formal class lessons, group or individual study and quiet contemplation. Eager volunteers were always ready to take visitors on a conducted tour and it was heartening to receive glowing reports of how courteous and informative the young guides were. Equally important was to ensure that the children, -and the older ones especially - were given an insight into the wider world, again through first-hand experience. At a heads' meeting, I made contact with a colleague who had established an environmental study area at his school in the Chilterns and a visit was arranged. This provided us with a stimulating experience and some useful practical ideas. This was followed by a weekend visit to the Forest of Dean for the older children, based at a youth hostel, which brought home to me the value to be gained from residential educational visits, which from then on became a regular feature of the summer term.

And so my second year in a Cotswold village school drew to a close and I faced once more the annual leave-taking by the fourth-year juniors that I had seen as routine in my earlier posts but now found something of a wrench. I had, after all, known and taught these children for two whole years and through them had been able to put into practice a good many of the ideas I had cherished for so long. Naturally enough, their thoughts as the last few days of term ebbed away were set on the future. They were ready to move on; no doubt during the first few weeks of the next school year, a few of them, clad in their new uniforms, would call in to relate how they were now 'doing' chemistry, physics, French and other subjects, the bolder ones embellishing their accounts with daring descriptions of the eccentricities of various teachers encountered. By the very nature of things, this was the way it would always be. In fact, were it otherwise, one could only conclude that the children had yet to adjust to this new stage in their education and that would be a cause for concern.

Even so, these children would be sadly missed. Like them, however, my thoughts had to be directed towards the future, which would no doubt be safe in the hands of the new fourth-year. That summer, as well as taking a welcome family holiday, and attending a course on the history of hedges, I set about discovering something of my Cotswold surroundings. Although by now a car owner, I soon realised that, as with the Peak District, the only true way to get to know the region intimately was to travel on foot. Starting in my immediate neighbourhood, the Evenlode valley, I began to explore the network of footpaths and bridleways, many of which were at that time unmarked and little used. And while birds and wild life generally remained foremost in my affections, the subtle charm of the landscape and the timeless beauty of the fashioned stone soon began to captivate me. Building a library of Cotswold books enhanced this attachment, especially the discovery of a lovingly-written book on my adopted village by an Oxford don who had resided there for almost half a century.

So although Derbyshire retained its hold on my affections, I began to establish an affinity with the Cotswolds which was to bring immense pleasure and satisfaction over the years in ways I could not possibly anticipate.

The nature reserve - early days.

The nature reserve - 15 years later.

Examining tracks and trails.

Investigating little owl roost.

Boys model making.

Girls model making.

Nature trail open day.

Nature trail open day.

The wood. Marking the paths.

The wood in winter.

Severn expedition. Nearing the source.

Severn expedition. Classroom display.

Gambian children. 1969.

Gambian village school. 1969.

Gambian beach scene.

Gambian teachers in the Cotswolds.

Chapter 12

One Saturday, round about dusk, soon after the start of the new term, we were enjoying a quiet evening when there was a loud knock on the door. It was Alan. My former pupil, who unlike several other July leavers, had not yet paid me a return visit, came to the point straight away.

'We're goin' crayfishin'', he announced. 'Loike t' come?'
I struggled to gather my thoughts. 'Why, yes – yes, I'd love to. I'll just get ready.'
'You'll need wellies', prompted Alan.
Soon we were stepping out across the green. I ventured to ask who the others were.
'Jus' me an' our Ant'ny an' our Andy', came the reply.

Anthony, of course, I knew of old, whereas Andy, I seemed to recall, was the youth who shattered the evening calm as he rode past at breakneck speed on his motor bike. But not this evening, apparently. Just then, two figures emerged from behind a tree on the edge of the green. My presence was acknowledged in a perfunctory fashion and soon we were making our way down the bridleway and over the stile leading to the river. The light was fading fast by now and there was an autumnal chill in the air. Patches of mist were already beginning to form ahead, masking familiar features. We advanced in silence, the only sound the distant 'kr-aak' of a moorhen.

Reaching the river bank at last, we drew up beneath the hollowed-out trunk of a leaning willow. Our equipment was laid out on the grass.
'Rioght, let's 'ave that bait then', demanded Andy.

Anthony promptly produced a plastic bag containing an evil-smelling mass of offal, which he and Alan began to dole out into a collection of perforated concave discs, about the size of dinner plates. These were then suspended, each by three strings, from long bamboo canes, and lowered into the water at about fifty-yard intervals as we made our way upstream. Andy also carried a long pole with a forked end, resembling a home-made clothes prop, which he used to keep the baited discs stable as they were lowered into the river.

It was dark by the time that the last of the dozen or so traps had been laid. Andy sat down on the bank, took out a packet of cigarettes and addressed me directly for the first time. 'Want one, Mr.......er....?' His voice trailed off uncertainly.
Alan was quick to the rescue. 'Mr Ottewell's 'is name – that's what we called 'im at school,' he volunteered, adding as an afterthought, '– but I 'spect you'd call 'im Gordon.'

After a steady walk back by torchlight to the point where the first trap had been lowered, Andy decided that enough time had passed for the catch to be raised. The cane, supported by the forked pole, was carefully lifted and swung round to the bank. Sure enough, an assortment of crayfish of varying size were revealed, groping over one another in their determination to consume every morsel of the bait. In moments, Andy's deft fingers had consigned the large specimens to a sack and had returned the smaller ones to the river.

The torch battery being almost on the point of giving out by now, Andy decreed that from then on it should be used only for sorting the catch. This meant that we had to pick our way along the bank in darkness – no easy task, with ditches, severed branches, molehills and cowpats lying in wait for the carelessly-placed boot. The others seemed untroubled by these obstacles; I, by contrast, stumbled along breathlessly behind.

We had reached one of the last of the traps and Anthony - who had taken it upon himself to land the previous catch - turned suddenly to me. 'Loike t' do this 'un?' he enquired abruptly. Gingerly I took hold of the bamboo road and with Alan's help slowly and carefully began to raise the trap. This entailed leaning over the bank at an alarming angle, for the trap had been lowered as far into the river as possible, leaving very little leverage. It broke surface at last and I began with trepidation to guide it towards the bank, my waist muscles tense under the strain.

'Want t' sort 'em an' all?' Anthony enquired, a note of challenge unmistakable in his voice as we surveyed the squirming contents in the feeble torchlight. I declined. Landing the catch was one thing; fumbling with it in virtual darkness was quite another. At length, the last trap was raised and the contents assigned to their respective fates. Andy slung the bag over his shoulder.

'Reckon there's a 'unnerd or more in yurr,' he said as we set off on the homeward plod across the hushed and shrouded meadows. '– feels loike it, anyroad.'

I asked Andy whether his fishing was confined to crayfish. 'Nah,' came the reply. 'Oi loikes goin' after trout best. Good sport, that is - not in this river though.' But surely trout fishing rights were jealously guarded? I ventured. 'That's as maybe,' Andy countered with a chuckle. 'They gotta catch yer first, ent they?'

Back at the village green, it was made clear that my invitation to join the brothers extended to a crayfish supper afterwards. Leading the way towards their home, Andy became talkative. 'By roights o' course, we should a' cooked 'em down boi th' river an washed 'em down wi' beer,' he confided. 'That's what me an' moi da' used t' do, anyroad.' He indicated his younger brothers. ''course these two are a bit young for that yet.'

We kicked off our wellingtons on the kitchen step and padded in stockinged feet indoors. Blinking in the glare of the light, I was introduced to the boys' smiling mother, who I had met previously only as a parent at open evenings, and who in anticipation of our return, had an immense saucepan-full of water simmering on the stove. The contents of the sack were unceremoniously tipped into the pan and eventually Andy - who had supervised the cooking while his mother laid the table - proclaimed that the crayfish were ready to eat. The hissing pan was taken from the stove and a generous plateful of white and sunset-tinted crayfish was placed before me. I was then initiated into the art of extracting the edible parts – chiefly flesh from the legs – and the meal got under way. We ate ravenously, the crayfish supplemented by bread and washed down by cans of shandy, except for Alan, who with reluctance was compelled to settle for coke.

At last, sated, I thanked my hosts and rose to leave. Andy followed me to the door. 'Next toime we'll leave th' kids be'oind,' he promised. 'Boil th 'catch down boi th' river on a wood foire an' tek plenty o' cans o' beer. Taste even be'er loike that.'

The course on the history of hedges I attended during the holidays was a revelation. Hedgerows had been part of my life from early boyhood. I had taken them for granted, giving no thought to their origins, age or purpose, while at the same time vaguely regretting their passing from the scene when the fields around the village had been ravaged by opencast mining. Now, however, I began to see hedges in an entirely new light. They had served, I now knew, as stock-proof boundaries for centuries. Until recent years, they had been managed by traditional methods according to region.

The oldest hedges comprised up to a dozen species of trees and woody shrubs, not to mention a host of flowering and non-flowering plants. Their value as wildlife corridors I already appreciated and I was all too aware that the widespread practice of hedge-removal posed a serious threat to the lowland countryside.

So that when I saw Tom Elton laying a hedge near the school one late autumn afternoon, I stopped to watch, learn and admire his handiwork. Here was a man carrying out a traditional craft, using simple tools and producing something both useful and pleasing to the eye. I asked if he'd mind me bringing a group of children to watch and although he raised no objection, I sensed that he wasn't altogether convinced of the link between what he saw as a routine seasonal task and the education of young children. From my point of view, the half-hour we devoted to watching Tom hedgelaying was time well spent. Clearly self-conscious at first, Tom soon entered into the spirit of the exercise and dealt with the many questions raised with patience and good humour.

'Why are you cutting the hedge?'

'Because if I didn't, it would grow untidy and sprawl everywhere and not do its job properly.'

'Won't it kill the hedge, chopping it like that?'

'No, because I'm leaving the strongest shoots and weaving them into the hedge so that they'll grow and fill the gaps next spring.'

'If you're not careful, there won't be anywhere for the birds to build their nests.'

'Birds prefer thick hedges to nest in. Cutting a hedge like I'm doing makes it grow nice and thick. Come and look at it again next spring - then you'll see what I mean.'

As though to prove his point, Tom showed his young audience an old nest, cleverly tucked away in the section of hedge at which he was working. 'It's easier for nest-robbers – crows and magpies – to find nests in untidy, gappy hedges. It's harder for them to rob nests hidden in thick hedges, like this one will be.'

We thanked Tom and headed back to school. Lively discussion ensued. Tom had allowed the children to examine his billhook and slasher and there was a general feeling of amazement that such an enormous task was accomplished with such simple tools. 'I'm going to be a hedge-cutter when I grow up', Ian proclaimed. I enjoyed a quiet chuckle at the thought of how his affluent, ambitious parents would have reacted - their sights were set already on university and the professions for their son.

Prompted by knowledge gained on my course and further stimulated by our session with Tom Elton, I now began to look at hedges more closely. I knew already that the village open fields had been enclosed as recently as the 1850s, and that in common with other enclosures of that period, the hedges consisted almost exclusively of hawthorn. However, I had also learned that parish boundary hedges were often much older and species-rich than other hedges and that county boundary hedges, if present, were likely to be the oldest of all, dating from Saxon times.

As luck would have it, the village lay close to such a county boundary and I was delighted to discover that not only was a considerable length of the boundary hedge accessible from the road but it displayed the two chief features – curvature and the presence of mature trees – said to characterise such ancient boundaries. Enquiries revealed that the hedge formed part of a local estate, one of the employees of which was a parent of children at the school. He approached the agent on my behalf and permission was granted for me to survey the hedge, with a view to carrying out a detailed study with the children the following summer.

My reconnaissance confirmed all that I had hoped for. Allowing for the absence of leaves - thus preventing me from identifying with certainty all the woody plants present - it was immediately apparent that this hedge was a textbook example of the type described on my course and would make an ideal subject for study when in full leaf the following year.

It was but a small step from the subject of hedges to that of the fields which they enclosed. During our interview with Tom Elton, he had referred in passing to the names of certain of his fields and this had awakened the children's interest in the subject. Having recently been involved in thinking up names for the paths and other features of our nature reserve, they were curious to know how such names as Birdsmoor, Washmarsh, Henslade, Varnels, Yantel, Buttocks Lake, and Dining Acres came to be given to fields. Although we could make intelligent guesses at the origins of some of these, others remained a mystery and lead to much, often humorous, speculation.

I happened to mention the subject to Sid Hopkins one afternoon when he called to check the boiler. Sid had been a pupil at the school in its all-age era in the 1920s and could recall the then headmaster carrying out a local study with the seniors, which culminated in the marking of all the village fields on a large linen map. Was there any chance that it would still be around somewhere, I speculated.

'Up there in th' glory'ole, I shouldn't wonder,' Sid said with an upward tilt of the head. 'That's where everythin' used to end up. More junk up there than in Steptoe's yard.'

And so, one evening soon afterwards, clad in my gardening clothes, and with his wife steadying the ladder, I followed Sid up through the trapdoor and into the dust-laden, cobweb-hung darkness of the school loft. It took one sweep of the torch beam to confirm the truth of Sid's description. The loft was strewn with clutter of every imaginable kind – broken furniture, some of it bordering on the antique; boxes of ancient textbooks; moth-eaten stage costume; scraps of painted scenery; weaving looms – and lying with a bundle of other, smaller maps and charts in a recess under the eaves – a long cylindrical object on protruding wooden rollers.

'That's it!' Sid announced triumphantly. 'Thought it'd be up 'ere. No mistakin' it – ole Stanford 'isself made th' rollers.'

Amazingly, the map was in a surprisingly good state of repair. It dated from 1928, the year in which the county had promoted a village study project, and great pains had been taken with the accuracy and presentation. To my delight, the acreages and names of all the fields were clearly marked. As we were carefully cleaning off the accumulated dust and grime, I asked Sid if he could remember what part he had played in its making.

'None – none whatever!' came the reply, followed by a hollow laugh. 'The ole bugger wouldn't let me nor moi mates nowhere near. Said we'd 'ave made a pig's ear of it.' Again the hollow laugh. ' – an' we prob'ly would 'ave too!'

Cleaned up and carefully suspended from the wall, the map provided a great deal of interest, revealing as it did not only the field names but other details, down to the positions of prominent trees. It occurred to me how useful it would have been during our work on maps in my first year at the school. At least I had satisfied myself that nothing else of value lay gathering dust in the gloom above our heads.

Sid's reference to his own schooldays prompted me to dip into the school logbooks, and especially at the period, some forty years earlier, when our map had been drawn. Opening these formidable-looking volumes previously, I had tended to confine myself to skimming through the Victorian era, when payment by results was the norm and the visits of Her Majesty's Inspectors were awaited with dread. What were the teachers really like, I wondered? By reading between the lines, it was possible to get some idea of their diverse characters, but much remained pure speculation.

I studied the entries penned by Sid's headmaster at the time the map was drawn. To judge from his daily jottings, he ran a good school; was firm yet fair; was receptive to new ideas and was both intelligent and articulate. And yet - in Sid's memory at least - he emerged as something of a tyrant. I decided to pursue the matter further with Sid at the next opportunity. Yes, he conceded, Mr. Stanford had been a clever man - and practical too. But strict with it – a dab-hand with the cane. Believed in striking first and asking questions afterwards. Retired to Weston-super-Mare eventually. Suddenly, Sid's face creased into a grin. 'Seed 'im once when oi were drivin' through Wes'on. Crossin th' road, 'e was. Doddery ole fella boi then.'

'Did you stop for a word?' I asked.

'No fear – put m' foot down on th' 'cellerator. Missed the bugger though.' came the reply.

85

Chapter 13

That winter, I spent every available moment reading everything I could lay my hands on relating to the village, and in particular, to its schools, the present one and the building, formerly the rector's tithe barn, it had replaced in 1912. A systematic study of the school's log books, hitherto merely opened at random, now brought rich rewards. The oldest of these formidable-looking volumes, with its black outer cover and richly marbled inside, dated back to 1873, and contained the often lengthy yet invariably revealing entries made by the then headmaster, William Jackson, recorded in immaculate copperplate. Jackson was in charge of the school from its opening in 1858 until his retirement in 1902, and was not only the longest-serving head by far but his entries gave a deeper insight into the life of the school – and indirectly into that of the village – than the combined entries of all his successors.

I had no means of knowing what fate had befallen the school's first log book, covering the years 1858 – 1872, but if the oldest surviving book was anything to go by, it must have been an invaluable source of information. As it was, a detailed study of Jackson's entries made over the last 29 years of his reign provided me with a clear impression of a man who, despite countless difficulties, was both a dedicated teacher and a pillar of the village community.

This view was later borne out by my reading of a book on the village published after Jackson's death by the Oxford don, a resident for many years, mentioned earlier. This work, written with an engaging blend of erudition and affection and in a style reminiscent of Gilbert White's unsurpassed work on Selborne, contained an intriguing impression of William Jackson:

Not long before I first knew the village, a schoolmaster had been procured from a training college, young smart, alert, and certificated. He was an optimist; he thoroughly believed in himself and his work, and he did in truth very well as things were done then.........He was a mighty person in the village, and no one who wanted official help, ever thought of applying to anyone else.'

This self-belief is immediately evident from the log book's very first entry:

March 10th 1873: Sent for the mother of Rose Poyser and complained to her of Rose's misconduct, she having been saucy when corrected by the pupil teacher. Mrs Poyser wished me to administer the cane, but I did not do so, but reproved her publicly in school.

A year later, another incident involving a girl's misbehaviour, provides further evidence of Mr Jackson's unflinching belief in his own judgment:

May 25th 1874: This morning Charlotte Findley, a girl of the 3rd standard, showed an exhibition of her very violent temper, after a reproof by the master, who refused to admit her to her class until she made him an apology. It was eleven o'clock before she recovered herself to make the apology, which, having done, she was forgiven. Her stubbornness, and the master's forbearance, may possibly do both her and her schoolfellows some good.

Four years later, Jackson is still striving to raise the moral tone, even to the point of disrupting the normally rigidly prescriptive timetable:

May 17th 1878: Spent some time investigating a lie which was conclusively brought home to Percy Woolliams, whom I punished severely and shall see his parents on the matter tonight. Gave an extra lesson to the higher standards in place of geography on 'Truthfulness.'

In contrast, numerous entries indicate Jackson's tolerance and approachability, despite the rigours imposed by regular visits by H.M. Inspectors, the constant outbreaks of infectious diseases and the cramped and insanitary condition of the school building:

January 23rd 1884: Master's birthday. The children asked for a holiday but were refused with a promise of one on a fine day.

December 23rd 1891: Closed school at 3.10pm to enable the children and teachers to enjoy an hour on the frozen floods.

January 1st 1900: New Year's greetings between teachers and scholars. Afterwards I gave a talk about the 19th century.

Numerous log book entries over the years concerned military drill carried out with the older boys by a Captain (later Colonel) Barrow. Later, I learned that this gentleman, the son of Sir John Barrow, Secretary to the Admiralty and a wealthy bachelor, had retired to the village in the 1860s and concerned at the unruly behaviour of some of the local lads, had established his own regiment of drill boys, dressed in smart uniforms and equipped with model rifles. Despite having military connections, it was said that Barrow never attained officer rank, let alone that of captain, and his later elevation to colonel was self-promotion. However, he was well known for his generosity and there was no shortage of recruits for his private army.

I could only speculate how the worthy colonel became involved in the life of the school; what was clear was that the drill boys spent many school hours marching to neighbouring villages and taking part in various events and that the display they staged at the time of Her Majesty's Inspectors' visits met with whole-hearted approval. Later, I discovered that the self-styled colonel kept his own log books, which on his death were lodged in the Bodleian Library, and which on inspection contained a wealth of information about his eventful life, the village to which he retired, and page upon page of newspaper cuttings reporting world affairs.

Sadly, the departure of Mr Jackson was followed by a period of instability. Two head teachers, the first a mistress, stayed only briefly; the second seemed to have had a stand-up row with His Majesty's Inspector, judging by a heavily-erased entry in the log book, after which he apparently left the school in mid-term.

The year 1909 saw an end to this unhappy phase in the school's fortunes with the arrival as headmaster of William Ernest Henry Potter. This gentleman, recalled with a mixture of awe and downright loathing by a handful of elderly villagers, proceeded to take what must have been a failing school and in no time at all literally knock it into shape by imposing a code of discipline the harshness of which remained a talking point half a century after he left to serve in the great war. It was during the Potter years that the old school building was finally replaced by the new council school overlooking the village green, built to accommodate 120 children of all ages and in its time considered a model of its kind.

Not that the educational opportunities offered by this new teaching environment were allowed to go to Mr Potter's head, judging by the log book entries of that time. On the contrary, his sprawling script is given over almost exclusively to a record of the manifold transgressions of the pupils and to the interminable thrashings he administered to all and sundry who dared to incur his wrath.

Apart from the occasional entry relating to the achievements of the senior boys in the cultivation of vegetables in the new school garden, the one record of activity out of doors relates to a visit paid to see a military aeroplane, piloted by a local man, which had landed in a field close to the school.

It was during the war years, when in the absence of the headmaster, the school was left in the charge of a succession of temporary teachers, that the retired Oxford don before mentioned began to take an active interest in its welfare. As correspondent to the managers, he had for several years visited the school to check the registers, a ritual of the utmost importance at the time, and to listen to and comment upon the children's singing. Now, however, he gradually became involved, indirectly at first, in the teaching process. In a book of short essays published at the time, he described how after telling the older children that he would be absent from the village for some weeks, he invited them to note any incident relating to natural history during his absence, offering a prize for the most interesting account. There is no record of how many responses he received; all he revealed was that the prize was awarded to a boy who noted that he heard a cuckoo call repeatedly during a severe thunderstorm.

Later, the old don talked to the children about Shakespeare, illustrating his talk with short readings and pointing out that the great man had spent his boyhood 'but twenty miles away, a good day's walk or morning's cycle ride.......... I tried to make them feel that he really belonged to us, looked up at our hills from the Avon valley, spoke the same speech as our folk. I did not keep them much more than half an hour,' the don went on, 'and during that time I saw no sign of listlessness. I have since heard that one small boy, distinguished for his naughtiness, complained that I stopped too soon, but that may have been because the half hour was for him an idle one. It is possible, I hope, that some of these young ones will not entirely forget what I told them about the great hero of our countryside.'

Returning from war service, Mr Potter was promoted to the headmastership of a large school in a nearby town and for a time the village school experienced another unsettled phase. Fortunately, however, the new headmaster, to judge by his entries in the log book, was not only a dedicated teacher but brought with his skill an enlightened and compassionate nature utterly dissimilar from that of the dreaded Potter. The school flourished, discipline improved, the curriculum widened, and for the first time the outside world – the village, its history, its farms and its place in the local landscape – began to feature in the learning process. Here, I felt, was a kindred spirit, a man with whom I had a distinct affinity. True, there were problems, especially concerning some of the senior boys, reluctant pupils counting the days until they could exchange the classroom for the world of work, but such was Mr Cooke's enthusiasm for his calling that such minor irritants were never allowed to disrupt the overall wellbeing of the school.

An intriguing, yet all too brief glimpse into the lives of the young headmaster and his wife was revealed when I came across a book of the collected letters of an American novelist and former resident of the village, published after her early death by her husband, a literary critic. Writing to a close friend, she remarked: 'We have just had the school-master and his wife to high-tea; such a dear young couple; she is perfectly charming and oh, such taste in clothes! – on their tiny salary; the most harmonious and modish figure.'

Inevitably, promotion to a larger school was bound to tempt such a forward-looking and accomplished headmaster and this did indeed happen after a few years. His successor, the master recalled with grudging respect by Sid, remained for a far longer period, his reign extending almost to the second world war. Despite Sid's condemnation, I learned from other former pupils that Mr Stanford , though a strict disciplinarian, ran a reasonably good school, and skills learned by boys in his woodwork classes, in particular, were put to good use in later life.

How would future readers of the school log book judge me, I wondered as my reading brought me to the present day. Would what I wrote be a true reflection of my achievements? I could only hope so.

Chapter 14

Determined to avoid our disappointment of the previous spring, when our newly-sited tit boxes had failed to attract any occupants, we set to work during the winter months constructing new boxes and modifying old ones in plenty of time for the coming breeding season. After consulting various books and RSPB pamphlets, we extended our range from enclosed boxes for tits to include open-fronted ones for robins and flycatchers and a special box intended for tawny owls, in the hope that Oliver had remained in the vicinity and had found a mate. This box was far too large for the nature reserve but Tom Elton allowed us to fix it in a nearby tree on his land.

Making these boxes was a valuable interdisciplinary exercise, involving accurate measuring, the competent use of woodwork tools and a good deal of patient cooperation between groups of children. We decided to fit hinged lids to some of the enclosed boxes, to enable us to open them to count the eggs and young, although some of the girls expressed misgivings about this, arguing that sitting birds should be left free of disturbance. As Jenny put it:

'How would your mum like it if a giant kept peering in at her when she was feeding her baby?'

Eventually a compromise was agreed upon; the hinged lids would be opened at well-spaced intervals, and then only by one person and in my presence. Later, we adopted a means of inspecting the contents of the boxes without the need to climb up and peer inside. This involved propping open the overhanging lid with a wooden pole and viewing the interior using a small mirror attached to a bamboo cane.

With our nest boxes in place – their numbers offering a bewildering choice to the local bird population – we turned our attention to nests in general. Someone brought in a section of hollow tree trunk containing a woodpecker hole and this provided the incentive for other contributors. Nests of all shapes and sizes appeared, including some with infertile eggs still inside. An examination of the materials used in the construction of these nests revealed a few surprises; apart from the usual twigs, grasses, moss, feathers and hair, we discovered pieces of plastic, silver foil, coloured thread and sweet-wrappers all interwoven in the structure.

The logical next step was to try our hand at nest-building ourselves, using similar materials to those employed by the birds. Much effort was expended and great pains taken, with the predictable outcome that the shapeless and fragile results of our endeavours served to increase the children's wonder that, equipped only with a beak, birds managed to create such beautiful, and above all, functional homes in which to raise their young.

With the onset of what proved to be a lengthy spell of severe weather, our bird table became the scene of constant activity. Situated in a good position for viewing, it allowed the children to learn to identify our common resident birds at close quarters. Once familiar with the birds themselves, we began to study the distinctive habits of individual species, differentiating between the walkers and the hoppers, the agile, the bold, the timid, the aggressive, and so on. We then turned our attention to food preferences, weighing the quantities of different foods put out and repeating the exercise with the leftovers at the end of the school day.

A visit to the Severn Wildfowl Trust grounds at Slimbridge, and in particular the chance to watch wintering swans, geese and ducks from a hide, prompted Paul and Steven to investigate the possibilities of constructing their own hide in preparation for observing their tit box, situated in an apple tree in the school orchard, in the coming spring. Eventually they hit upon the idea of converting an old blackboard easel, which they covered with sheets of cardboard, leaving a gap at eye level. A generous coat of green paint was then applied and the hide stored away in a corner of the classroom ready for use later. Meanwhile I had decided to order a pair of lightweight binoculars. These would enable a detailed study to be made of the food preferences of the occupants of our nest boxes, their use being a special privilege for two older children, appointed as nature wardens on a weekly rota system. Among the lunchtime duties allocated to the wardens were topping-up the pond and bog garden, watering needy plants, keeping an eye on the nature reserve generally and showing round visitors. Thus prepared, we awaited the arrival of spring with eager anticipation.

As the first of April rarely fell during term-time, the opportunity to play an April fool trick on the children seldom occurred. This spring, however, the school was in session on the day and guessing that I would be subjected to plenty of tricks, I decided to plan my own trick in advance.

I had discovered amongst the junk in the school house garage an air raid warden's helmet, left behind presumably by a previous head. After lining it with straw, I suspended it from the garage ceiling and placed in it an ostrich's egg given me by a retired teacher. When All Fools' Day finally arrived, and after enduring numerous predictable efforts from the children, I allowed the high spiritedness to subside before announcing that I had discovered the nest of a rare bird in my garage and that those children who promised to approach on tiptoe and without speaking could accompany me to see it. Needless to say, everyone pledged solemnly to abide by these conditions and soon a silent queue had formed outside the rear garage door to be allowed inside, one at a time, for a quick peep before returning to the classroom through the main door.

Rejoining the class with the last pupil, I was met with pandemonium. A handful of the older boys, quick to spot the joke, were pouring scorn on other children who had failed to do so, while others, although aware that I had tried to outwit them, were deep in a noisy argument about which bird had produced the giant egg.

At morning break, Jean, on learning the cause of the excitement in the next classroom, asked if her children could share the experience. I was told later that the exercise gave rise to a great deal of speculation as the little ones were lifted up to peer over the brim of the 'nest' to see the strange egg laid by the mystery bird.

The tattoo of knocking on the door that early spring Saturday morning was both loud and insistent. Opening it, I was confronted by a band of older junior boys, led by Graham, triumphantly holding a writhing grass snake for my inspection. With everyone determined to have his say, it took some time for me to grasp the full story:
'We found it on the old railway embankment.'
'It didn't look very happy where it was - .'
'And so we thought we'd bring it to you.'
'So it can be set free in the nature reserve.'
' 'Cos we know it'll be safe there.'

I thanked them and endeavoured to produce a smile of gratitude. So much for my attempts to instil the conservation ethic; my patient explanation of why we had created suitable habitat for wild creatures in the hope that in time that they would colonise it, etc. Yet how could I possibly blame these lads for trying to speed up the process? After all, waiting hopefully doesn't come naturally to young children; theirs is a world of instant action, in which impulse reigns. So although I knew that I should have demanded that they returned the snake to its chosen habitat, I simply hadn't the heart. Instead, I donned my coat and shoes, grabbed a sheet of corrugated iron I had earmarked for another purpose, and led the way to the reserve, where the creature was carefully placed under its protective cover, in the hope that it would find its new abode congenial.

Speculation was rife on Monday morning. Would the snake still be where we had released it? I resisted the numerous appeals to find out until lunchtime, when I allowed Graham, as finder, to take a careful peep, while the rest of us watched from a distance. With a gentle deliberation quite foreign to his nature, Graham raised the edge of the iron sheet and peered beneath. As he lowered it and turned to face us, his glum expression told its own tale. Back in the classroom, I tried yet again to convey the concept on which the creation of our nature reserve had been based, labouring the point that we must allow wild creatures to discover the reserve in their own time rather than attempt to introduce them ourselves.

The whereabouts of the snake was the main talking point for several days. Was it still somewhere in the nature reserve? Or had it slithered the half-mile or so back to its former haunts on the railway embankment? It was noticeable that despite my assurances that grass snakes were entirely harmless, a few children stepped with trepidation in the reserve for some time afterwards; snakes of any kind were still regarded with suspicion - dread even - and I learned later that this fear was exploited by some of the older boys, who recounted extravagant tales of the phenomenal size of this particular snake and credited it both with venomous and constriction powers.

Although the snake was never seen again, there was plenty of evidence that other creatures had begun to colonise our reserve. At least one pair of great diving beetles appeared in the pond, where their carnivorous larvae were quick to devour the tadpoles that emerged from frogspawn donated by a well-wisher. Later, dragonflies and damsel flies bred in the reeds by the pond margin and a host of smaller creatures – skaters, water boatmen, fresh-water shrimps and so on - provided endless interest to the small groups of children observing from the water's edge.

As spring advanced, we were delighted to discover that two pairs of blue tits had begun nesting in our boxes. One pair had chosen the box in the orchard and Paul and Steven, equipped with our newly-purchased binoculars, commenced regular observation from their hide, recording and timing the comings and goings of the birds. To the human eye, the sexes are identical so the boys could not differentiate between the parent birds but eventually, after hatching had taken place, they were able to confirm that both birds were feeding the young. This involved a shuttle service to and from a clump of hawthorns, on which a vast quantity of small dark caterpillars were feeding.

As in other years, I rose early on several mornings and set off cross the fields to hear the dawn chorus, which was at its best in the first weeks of May. I happened to mention this to the mother of two of the children, herself a nature lover, and although it was agreed that such an exercise was impractical for the children, we decided that as a second-best we could at least arrange an evening meeting for enthusiasts to listen to the dusk chorus in the school orchard. Accordingly, one Friday evening, a group of children and parents gathered beneath the trees as dusk drew near to wait and to listen. An hour or so later, with the light by now almost gone, we were still there, determined to establish which of the last two performers in the nocturne – robin and song thrush – would even-tually bring the performance to an end. Later still - with the last liquid notes of the robin alone punctuating the silent night - we headed for home, contented at having shared a memorable expe-rience.

Chapter 15

As a direct result of our evening bird-song vigil towards the end of the previous term, the start of what promised to be an extremely busy summer term brought with it an offer of help that was to prove invaluable. Three mothers of junior pupils - friends who shared a genuine love of the countryside –volunteered to assist with our outdoor activities in any way I cared to suggest. I accepted with alacrity.

The first project on which I enlisted this assistance was the survey of the county boundary hedge. After several sessions spent in polishing up our identification skills to ensure that we could identify the main species likely to be found on the survey, we divided into four groups. We then marked out at random four 30-yard lengths in the recommended fashion and proceeded to count the different species of trees and woody shrubs in each section. Back in school, we presented our findings in table form:

Group 1	Group 2	Group 3	Group 4
Hawthorn	Hawthorn	Hawthorn	Hawthorn
Blackthorn	Blackthorn	Blackthorn	Blackthorn
Oak	Oak	Oak	Oak
Elm	Elm	Elm	Elm
Ash	Field Maple	Ash	Ash
Field Maple	Dogwood	Field Maple	Field Maple
Dogwood	Sycamore	Crab Apple	Dogwood
Crab Apple	Sallow	Hazel	Crab Apple
Hazel	Wild Privet	Holly	Hazel
	Guelder Rose	Spindle	Wild Privet
		Elder	Spindle
			Elder
			Wayfaring tree
Total: 9	Total: 10	Total: 11	Total: 13

According to information gained on my course, the age of a hedge could be arrived at by counting the number of different woody species within it and allowing each to represent one hundred years. Bearing in mind that the counties had come into being before the Norman Conquest, our species-count seemed to confirm that the hedge line (i.e. the boundary) was indeed of Saxon origin. One thousand years of history! Here was something that had eluded Mr Stanford and the children who had carried out the 1928 survey. We were elated.

Having dated the hedge, we turned our attention to the natural history in and around it. Bounded on either side by arable fields, it proved to be a valuable wildlife corridor, providing dense cover for nesting birds. Its ancient oaks offered congenial habitat for insects and its banks sustained such endearing wild flowers as violet, lesser celandine, herb robert, red campion and wild arum. All that remained was to send a copy of our findings to the agent of the estate, who had kindly made the project possible, together with a letter of thanks, signed by everyone who took part.

Bridges, and in particular the newly-opened Severn Bridge, captured our imagination later that term. Several children had been taken to see or to cross this exciting new engineering achievement and on a day visit, the whole class were able to view the spectacle and later to compare it with Brunel's equally impressive bridge spanning the Bristol Avon at Clifton. From bridges, it seemed a natural step to extend our studies to rivers and that June, with one of my parent-volunteers acting as driver, I took the fourth-year children on a long weekend minibus exploration of the Severn valley. We scaled Plynlimmon in swirling mist to find its elusive source and followed the youthful river through Welshpool to Shrewsbury. Stops at Roman Wroxeter and the noble ruins of Buildwas Abbey followed before we entered Coalbrookdale and clambered over the first iron bridge, built almost two centuries earlier by Abraham Darby. Bridgnorth, with its striking setting, tilting castle remains and funicular railway, provided yet further interest before we set off for home, viewing the Severn once more in its pride as it flowed beneath the mighty span of Worcester bridge.

The infant class too were involved in their own river study that term. Or at least, that was the way it turned out. Jean's original idea was to carry out a project on water generally, but as several of the older infants had brothers and sisters in the junior class, and interest in rivers was running high, she wisely 'went with the flow.' This shift of emphasis led her to concentrate on our local Thames tributary, the Evenlode, and the project culminated in a boat trip from Oxford along the Thames to Abingdon, which proved a great success.

Rivers and bridges therefore, were the dominant themes in our open day display as the term drew towards its close. A large-scale relief map of the Severn valley formed the centrepiece in the junior classroom together with model bridges of every imaginable kind, ranging from a simple log to a working model of a suspension bridge constructed between two chairs. Impressive art and written work was produced and displayed and the group that had taken part in the expedition to the Severn source enacted their own dramatic presentation of the adventure. The infants meanwhile were not to be outdone; parents and other visitors were invited to try simple water experiments and to listen to stories and prayers composed by the children on the water theme.

Two phone calls, received within days of each other shortly before school closed for the summer holiday, were to have far-reaching implications for the school in vastly different ways. The first of these was from the house-father of a nearby residential home for disadvantaged children, requesting an appointment to discuss the possible admission of a ten-year-old boy to the school in the following September. Having heard conflicting accounts about this establishment, I was naturally wary; however, I was assured at the interview that the boy, though lively, was essentially a rough diamond, who would soon settle into village school life. Still with serious misgivings, I eventually agreed to the admission. Surely, I told myself, however rough the diamond proved to be, between us we would be able to polish him into an acceptable state before too long.

The second call was from the agent of the estate on which we had carried out the hedgerow survey some weeks before. He apologised for not acknowledging our survey results and thank-you letters before but having only just got around to reading them was most impressed. In view of this, and of reports he had received from various sources concerning our creation of a school nature reserve, he wondered whether we would like to make use of a five-acre wood on the estate. It was a well- established mixed wood, somewhat overgrown in places but with plenty of scope for the kind of nature studies he imagined we wished to develop. Access was comparatively easy and it was ours to use exclusively if we so wished, for a couple of years at least. Was I interested? I gulped 'Yes, please!' One way or another, the new school year promised to be one to remember.

Chapter 16

It was the first morning of the new school year. I was busily preparing for the children's arrival when the peace was shattered as three of the upper junior girls burst in.

'Please sir, there's a boy swinging from a branch on the apple tree!'

'Yes sir. We told him to stop or we'd tell – but he wouldn't!'

'And he swore at us as well. He said - ,'

I didn't wait for Annette to repeat the expletive but hurried outside. A crowd of children stood motionless beneath the tree, staring upwards in amazement as a boy swung effortlessly from branch to branch above their heads. Seeing my approach, the spectators withdrew to a discreet distance. It required a sharp command from me to bring the performance to a conclusion and the performer down to earth. And so began our year-long association with Maurice – a year in which one so-called rough diamond managed to put everyone's patience, goodwill – sanity, even – to the test, and who, as far as the other children were concerned, might just as well have come to us direct from another planet.

Small, lithe, fresh-complexioned, Maurice had arrived at his Cotswold residential home shortly before from Middlesex, following the break-up of his parents' marriage. I never did discover much about his upbringing; his restless, impulsive and at times badly anti-social behaviour indicated a deeply disturbed early childhood but with no records or reports to consult, I was left to draw my own conclusions and to devise ways of integrating him into our school community accordingly. This task might have been easier in a more formal setting. However, our method of working involved the children in a good deal of moving around, albeit in a self-disciplined fashion, and to a child of Maurice's background, this must have seemed like the green light to flit aimlessly about, disrupting other children and being a nuisance generally.

And yet for all his hyperactivity and townee brashness, there was something distinctly likeable about Maurice. On a one-to-one basis I found that our rough diamond was both intelligent and imaginative (a plausible liar too, when the need arose) and that, hidden beneath the streetwise, flinty exterior lay a sensitive, even compassionate temperament that had somehow withstood the harsh indifference of early experience. The discovery of these redeeming qualities persuaded me - against my better judgment -to persevere with the task of integrating Maurice into the school, at the cost of much extra planning, energy and peace of mind, and with it the ever-present danger of devoting too much time to one child to the detriment of the rest.

For all their tolerance and apparent docility, I could hardly expect the children to endure Maurice's disruptive behaviour indefinitely without some form of reaction. For the first time since arriving at the school, I found myself having to calm heated emotions; intervene in potentially bitter quarrels and generally lay down the law - the one common factor in all this being the involvement to some degree of Maurice. Inevitably, however, there were times when I was prevented from carrying out my peace-keeping role and it was on one of these occasions that the children themselves took matters into their own hands and in doing so did us all a favour.

Responding to an urgent knock on my office door one lunch-time, I was confronted by an agitated playground supervisor, who begged me to intervene in a fight that was taking place in the far corner of the grounds. By the time I arrived on the scene, the other supervisor had managed to separate the combatants - Maurice and two other boys – all of whom, and Maurice especially, were tearful, subdued and dishevelled. I learned that Maurice had provoked the other two to such an extent that they had finally lost patience and, cheered on by their classmates, had set about their tormentor, ignoring the pleas of the supervisors in their desperation. It was clear that the outnumbered Maurice had had the worst of the encounter and while quietly remonstrating with all three in the privacy of my office, I kept the whole affair as low-key as possible, in the hope that it would soon be forgotten.

Which, in a way, it was. There were no more fights and as far as I could see, no grudges harboured. On the contrary, the physical confrontation cleared the air, and although Maurice continued to exasperate us all from time to time, from then onwards he began gradually to adjust to our ways, was accepted and befriended, and seemed to enjoy and benefit from his final primary school year.

I paid several visits to the wood before taking the children. It stood on rising ground to the north of the village, not far from the ancient parish boundary hedge and as our large-scale map revealed, was roughly triangular in outline. I approached diffidently at first, conscious of crossing private land and half-expecting a figure to loom up without warning to challenge my presence. For apart from the agent's phone call, I had no authorisation to be there and was all too aware that virtually all woodland for miles around was given over to pheasant rearing and anyone found trespassing, however, unwittingly, would be sent packing with dire warnings against repeating the offence.

There was clear evidence, in the form of rusting oil drums and the rickety remains of improvised shelters, that this wood too had once been devoted to raising game for the shooting fraternity. I soon discovered that a few pheasants still remained - safe, like the wood's other inhabitants, from the threat of the gun, for some time at least.

Once inside the wood, the outside world became instantly remote. Tall mature trees - a few veteran oaks, a beech and a sycamore or two, a clump of Douglas fir – rose above the other vegetation, while below, a tangle of smaller trees and bushes – ash, hawthorn, hazel, holly and elder among them – struggled for dominance. There was only one clearly defined path – a cart track, almost obliterated in places – extending through the middle of the wood. Otherwise the only obvious paths were those formed by wild creatures, weaving their way secretly beneath the bushes and scarcely passable, even for the smallest of children. Not that I intended allowing the children to wander indiscriminately anyway. Pleasant and instructive though that might be for some of the class – I had been reading BB's *Brendon Chase* and a few of the older boys in particular, identified strongly with the three young outlaws living in the wild – I intended using our visits, as with those to our nature reserve, as carefully planned learning opportunities. There would be scope for adventure, and fun too in due course, but bearing in mind that the exercise would involve the entire class of twenty-five, including the now more compliant but still occasionally volatile Maurice, I would need to proceed with caution.

Our first class visit, on a mild and mellow late autumn afternoon, was something of a revelation for all involved. A convoy of cars – my trio of helping mothers were again proving indispensable – conveyed us to the nearest point of entry and we gathered in a small clearing for a final briefing. For some children, this was obviously their first visit to a wood. Excitement, apprehension – fear, even – were all apparent as we set off along the track, pausing at intervals to peer upwards through the leafy canopy, to touch different textures of bark, to listen to the wind's murmur, or to attune to the atmosphere of the wood.

Questions were asked and answered, notes made and specimens collected. On the way back to the waiting cars, we paused to take in the view and to pick out landmarks and other features close at hand. It soon emerged that many of the children, including some of the older ones, though having travelled by car along this road many times before, had never had their attention directed to the extensive sweep of landscape visible from our nearest hill and in consequence were unfamiliar with so much of interest that it contained. As teachers, we often spoke of the need to widen children's horizons; here, literally, was an example of that need.

By now, the work we were doing in our local environment had been brought to the attention of a wider public. A steady stream of visitors - heads, inspectors, advisers and other interested parties – asked to be allowed to tour the nature reserve and I was invited to lead a number of field-study courses based at the school.

Meanwhile, the school itself was expanding. A new classroom had been built and a third full-time teacher appointed. This meant that instead of teaching the entire junior range, my class now comprised the two upper age groups, thus easing my teaching workload considerably. Ironically, I was now allocated a few hours of secretarial help, leaving me with more time to assess the progress of the school as a whole, as well as to plan ahead for what I intended to be a more expansive approach to learning, through which to relate our school to the wider world.

Chapter 17

Happily, that wider world - or at least part of it - was about to come to us. I had a phone call from Bill, the area primary adviser, who had returned recently from establishing a link between the county and the tiny former West African colony of the Gambia, asking if he could bring a Gambian education officer to see the school. I promptly agreed and a few days later we were delighted to welcome a beaming, bubbly African lady into our midst, who wasted no time in getting involved with the children and was quick to appreciate how and why we placed the local environment at the hub of our curriculum.

Excitement ran high as our guest was escorted first round the nature reserve and then on a tour of the village, during which she was persuaded to sample wild blackberries; inspect a length of Tom Elton's newly-laid hedge; watch our widely-acclaimed blacksmith at work on wrought-iron gates; and see the rare medieval chimney perched high on the roof of Manor Cottages. Back in school, the children listened with wonder at our visitor's lively description of Gambian wild life and especially of the day-to-day lives of village children in that distant country. It was agreed that on her return home, the officer would try to arrange for our school to be twinned with a Gambian school of a similar size so that the children would be able to correspond with one another. All too soon, the time came for our charming visitor to depart .She was given a rapturous farewell and we made our way back into school with the happenings of a memorable afternoon on everyone's lips.

Soon afterwards, we had another welcome visitor. The young wife of an officer at the nearby RAF base, and herself a qualified teacher, she called to offer her services in a voluntary capacity for a couple of terms and expressed particular interest in our work on the local environment, adding as an afterthought that her husband was involved with the base weather station. Here were two valuable opportunities for the price of one and I grasped both eagerly. For some time I had been trying to find a way of reviving interest in our daily weather recording which, to some of the children at least, tended to be seen rather as a chore. Here was a chance to give the exercise a fresh impetus. And so, on a blustery late-autumn day, a coach-load of children arrived at the gates of the base for what proved to be a most absorbing and instructive visit. Allowing for the sophistication of the recording instruments, the children were quick to spot similarities between a real working weather station and our own modest affair and were only too ready to try their hand at operating various instruments under the guiding hands of their uniformed instructors. From the weather station we were escorted to the control tower, where we were able to see the nerve-centre of the base in operation and to gaze in awe at the quiet, efficient way in which the pilots of the planes that skimmed over our heads daily were trained in take-off and landing procedures.

Back at school, and with the autumn term by now well advanced, I decided that the best way in which we could make full use of our teacher-volunteer's remaining time with us would be to attempt a detailed survey of 'our' wood. Two of the older boys, Paul and Matthew, had already revealed an aptitude for practical mathematics and it was but a short step to revive interest in my predecessor's home-made theodolite and to carry out a few practice exercises before embarking on the real thing. The large-scale plan that resulted from our efforts that autumn was, to say the least, impressive. For as well as being mathematically accurate, it recorded the whereabouts of the principal trees, the distribution of the various species of ground vegetation and, as with our nature reserve, the names we had given to the paths. Also included were the locations at which various birds had been sighted – the most exciting being a female sparrow hawk – and the positions of fox and badger holes.

As with time spent with previous groups of children in the nature reserve, our woodland visits produced plenty of lively and imaginative art and written work. By happy coincidence, the first snow of the winter fell soon after I had read to the class the chapter in BB's *Brendon Chase* in which the three young outlaws experience the rigours of life in a snowbound forest; nothing daunted, we decided to set off over the whitened fields to discover for ourselves the magic of a wood under snow. After marvelling at the transformation that had taken place in our familiar haunts, we set about examining the various tracks left on the snow-dusted woodland floor, an exercise that led to much close observation and reasoned argument.

Before setting off back to school, we gathered in a clearing and I read a selection of poetry on the subject of snow. Longfellow's short poem of that name struck a responsive chord but Robert Frost's *Stopping by Woods on a Snowy Evening* made an even greater impact and prompted me to share more of his homespun yet deceptively thought-provoking verse with the children in the weeks that followed.

As spring approached, it was resolved that we would lay out our own nature trail in the school grounds and nature reserve and invite parents, school managers and villagers to see for themselves exactly what we had accomplished in our local environmental studies. The result was a number of open afternoons, in which all the children were involved - manning displays, presenting short talks and demonstrations and acting as guides around the trail itself. The response was gratifying and the positive feedback that resulted provided welcome encouragement to children and staff alike. On completing his tour under the guidance of a nine-year-old girl, one visitor - a distinguished writer on ornithology and vice president of the county naturalists' trust - expressed his delight at the occasion and remarked in an aside that as his young guide was showing him a buttercup, he had caught a glimpse of a lesser-spotted woodpecker, the first he had seen in the area.

Yet another cause for satisfaction was the winning-round of one of the few parents who had hitherto been openly critical of time spent in learning out of doors. The mother of a bright ten-year-old girl, she and her academic husband had moved into a large house in the village two terms previously and it was made clear to me at the outset that we were very much on trial. Since then, I had sensed that her misgivings remained, a view confirmed by remarks made by other professional-class parents, to the effect that in conversation at the school gate she had expressed dissatisfaction at what she considered our undue emphasis on outdoor activities.

I was aware during her visit on one of the open afternoons that she was subjecting the work on display to critical examination, paying particular attention to her daughter's study of the life cycle of the poplar hawk moth. It was not until several days later, however, that she made a point of coming to see me to express her satisfaction with what we were doing and to enthuse about her daughter's love of the work and enjoyment of school generally.

My own love of wild life, and especially birds, continued to provide immense pleasure. I had by now discovered that the Oxford don, who had lived in the village for many years, had not only written a book about it but was also a pioneer ornithologist, whose books on birds were ranked among the finest of the Victorian period. To my delight, I found that many of the sightings referred to in these volumes related to specific fields, woods and osier beds in and around the village. This knowledge provided an added incentive to my walks and in time I was able to establish what changes in the distribution of our resident and spring-visiting birds had taken place since the turn of the century.

Inspired by my reading, on many occasions that spring, I set off across the fields, either to our wood or to another, larger tract of woodland nearby, to listen to the dawn chorus and to familiarise myself with the songs of the individual performers. In time, these early morning sorties brought their reward; I was able to differentiate not only between the common resident birds but by patient listening managed to identify the more subtle songs of the migrant warblers. One morning, having driven to a more distant location, I returned to the car to find a police car parked alongside. If, as I suspected, the two occupants had hoped to catch a poacher red-handed, they did a pretty convincing job of concealing their disappointment and we parted with friendly banter.

Soon afterwards, I was told that a nightingale - a bird I had long sought in vain - had been heard in full song in a blackthorn thicket a few miles from the village. My visit to the spot late that same evening met with immediate success; as though on cue, the bird began its song as the nearby church clock struck eleven, and it was close on midnight by the time I dragged myself away from its virtuoso performance. Some time was to elapse before I caught my first and all-too-brief sighting of this skulking and unremarkable- looking little bird but the exhilaration I experienced on hearing its song for the first time is etched indelibly on my memory.

Later that year I had the opportunity to revive the memory of the don whose writings had provided me with so much pleasure. As the fiftieth anniversary of his death approached, I read several of his *Tales of the Birds* to the children, while at the same time launching an appeal for books, letters, photographs, personal recollections and any other items relating to him to enable me to stage a small exhibition at the appropriate time.

To my pleasant surprise, the response was most encouraging; my letter in an Oxford newspaper, in particular, yielding promises of a great deal of material, including the loan of a painting of the don displayed above high table in his former college.

One story in particular appealed to the children. Entitled 'A Debate in an Orchard', its setting was obviously our village and it featured an imagined dialogue between the local blackbird, robin, blue tit and sparrow, joined later by a passing swallow and other birds and concerned the complex relationship between birds and man. The story lent itself to dramatisation and the children performed the resulting sketch with enthusiasm as part of what became a full-blown event, including a selection of readings from the don's writings given to an appreciative audience by a group of volunteers.

That spring had one last achievement - of a sort - to offer. My lifelong love of cricket, though long since dormant, had never altogether expired and I had from time to time watched the youthful village team do battle on the attractive little ground in the shade of the church tower. At the suggestion of the elder brother of a former pupil, I agreed to turn my arm over at an evening net practice and to my surprise was invited to play in the home match on the following Saturday. Overawed somewhat to find myself in the company of a team comprising chiefly raw-boned young men, all of whom appeared to use a bat as a bludgeon and to bowl with unabashed if ill-directed venom, I found myself walking apprehensively to the wicket at number nine. Fortunately, the earlier batsmen had already flayed some lacklustre bowling and little depended on my efforts, which was just as well, as I managed only a couple of streaky singles before my middle stump was uprooted by a rare well-directed delivery.

The visitors, we discovered, were little better with the bat than with the ball and wickets soon began to tumble with monotonous regularity to our ferocious opening pair of bowlers. I had with mixed feelings reconciled myself to not being called upon to bowl but at the fall of the ninth wicket, and with victory a foregone conclusion, the captain tossed me the ball and invited me to try my luck .My first ball - and as I recall, the first genuinely slow delivery of the entire match - was a wretched long-hop, which to my relief the number eleven batsman lofted obligingly into the safe hands of mid -on. The game was won. As we trooped pavilion- wards to the muted applause of the half-dozen or so spectators, the youthful captain gave me a sheepish sidelong grin.

'Thanks for helpin' us out. We'll ask you again – sometime.' Needless to say, he never did. But at least I claimed a wicket with the last - and probably the worst - ball I ever bowled.

Chapter 18

Our residential field study expeditions had by now become an integral feature of the summer term. I had been told of an especially welcoming youth hostel, complete with workroom, situated between the Quantock Hills and Bridgwater Bay in a part of Somerset of which Margaret and I cherished happy memories of family holidays and of our honeymoon. A short visit confirmed its suitability; the warden and his wife were a delightful couple and I had no hesitation in booking then and there for our next study destination.

We had a marvellous week. The children carried out simple ecological surveys, collected fossils and enjoyed a ride on the local steam railway. We followed up each day's expedition in the workroom, writing up notes, making drawings of finds and presenting short talks on the various discoveries that took our fancy. The warden and his wife took a personal interest in our activities and it was agreed that they would be guests of honour on our final evening, when we intended to mount a display of all that we had accomplished.

It so happened that there were only a few other guests at the hostel during our stay; however, we were informed that another school party would be arriving in time for the evening meal on our final day but that this would not affect us, as their stay was to be a short one that would not involve use of the workroom.

Our itinerary on the final morning involved a short drive in the minibus to the approach to a steeply wooded combe, along which we intended to walk, returning to our starting point by a different route. We had walked only a short distance when Eric, one of the few keen-eyed country boys of the old-fashioned kind, let out a whoop of excitement.

'Look – look at that!'

All eyes turned in the direction of Eric's pointing finger. There, wedged between the tangle of tree roots a short distance up the steeply sloping bank was - a cauliflower, and a monster one at that.

Breathlessly, we scrambled up the bank to examine our prize.

'It's a cauliflower!'

'Course it is – anybody can see that.'

'It's a whopper – biggest I've ever seen!'

'Who does it belong to?'

'Must have fallen off a lorry.'

'How did it get here, sir?'

I had to confess that I had no idea. For although a minor road ran along the winding ridge above, it was little frequented, serving only to link two remote villages which lay slumbering in the hazy distance. My deliberations were cut short by Barry, who after conducting a quick survey of the party's food preferences, announced that as a majority of the group liked the taste of cauliflower, he proposed that we should take it back to the hostel and give it to the warden's wife.

A troubled frown crossed Julie's face. 'It's not ours to take though, is it?' she said stoutly. ''It'd be stealing, really, wouldn't it, in a way?'

'Finders keepers,' one of the boys mumbled.

A heated argument on the ethics of Barry's idea followed. Julie's stance clearly found favour among most of the girls. The ensuing stalemate was finally ended by Eric, who as finder was listened to by both sides in respectful silence.

'Unless it's eaten soon, it'll go bad,' he pronounced solemnly. 'I vote that if it's still here when it's time for us to go, we take it back with us.' Looking round at me inquiringly and hearing no objection, it was resolved to carry out Eric's suggestion.

'Spect the warden's wife 'll be glad of it,' Nicola observed, her staunch support of Julie's moral objections giving way to the logic

of her practical nature. 'Save her having to buy vegetables.'
Clive's remark that as we were leaving for home on the following day, the cauliflower would need to be cooked for the evening meal to avoid being devoured by 'that lot from the other school' was generally considered to be in doubtful taste. I pointed out that although the cauliflower appeared large enough to feed both parties, we couldn't reasonably expect the warden's wife to change her plans for the evening meal at short notice, but that no doubt she would do her best in the circumstances.

Despite all my careful planning, there was a distinct air of anti-climax about our afternoon's fieldwork. The mapping, measuring and recording were all carried out dutifully enough, but it was quite clear from snatches of overheard whispers that the children's minds were on other things. When at last the time came to return to the minibus, the feeling of expectancy was approaching fever pitch, so much so that I had to restrain some of the boys from breaking into a run. There was general relief when we spotted the cauliflower lying exactly as we'd left it. Led by Eric, the boys swarmed up the bank and returned with the giant vegetable, which was borne in triumph to the minibus.

Back at the hostel, the warden's wife managed a brave smile as the cauliflower was conveyed into her kitchen. ''Course we don't expect you to cook it tonight – not if it's not possible,' Eric assured her.
'No. It might just keep until tomorrow – after we've gone,' added Barry with meaning.
The warden's wife said she would see what she could do.

Speculation was rife as we took our places at the table. Eric, collecting a third helping of soup at the hatch, swung round to us with an ecstatic grin as the warden's wife answered his inevitable question in the affirmative.
'It's cauliflower next course!' he announced triumphantly. A spontaneous cheer echoed round the room. The faces of the children

in the other party showed distinct apprehension, which Eric's explanation to their teacher that he had found it under a tree miles from anywhere did little to relieve.

The cauliflower proved sufficient to feed everyone, and the story of its discovery figured prominently in written accounts, drawings and last-minute postcards to relatives and friends. A song in its praise was composed and sung with gusto on our homeward journey and the story gleefully retold at the follow-up evening for parents held later back at school.

'I just can't understand our Julie,' her mother confided as we chatted at the end of the meeting. 'She 's always turned up her nose whenever I serve cauliflower at home, yet here she is, writing about devouring two huge helpings of the stuff. I give up!'

I never ceased to be amazed at the criteria applied by so-called discerning parents when deciding whether or not to place their offspring in our school. Such parents, more often than not residing outside our catchment area, invariably began our interview by congratulating me on our reputation. To begin with, I accepted this remark as some kind of confirmation, vindication even, that our aims not only met with general approval but were fully understood. Gradually, however, it became clear that our so-called reputation meant different things to different parents. On the one hand, a number of these parents informed me that their reason for seeking their child's admission was that they had heard that the school was conducted on traditional lines, whereas others gave as their reason our supposed rejection of formal teaching in favour of complete reliance on informal methods. In truth, of course, we belonged to neither camp, but made use of a mix of styles, as did a good many village schools across the county, and for that matter, the country as a whole.

Needless to say, the clearing-away of these misconceptions led to some prospective parents looking elsewhere for a school that offered what they sought. To my pleasant surprise, however, a good number, having seen for themselves how we worked, decided to place their offspring in our care. One such couple, a titled family from a nearby village, enrolled their son in the infant class, where he remained before entering his prep school at the junior stage. During his time with us, his best friend was a village boy from a humble background and it became a familiar sight at the end of the school day to see the two friends clamber aboard the chauffeur-driven estate car, bound for tea at the manor.

The uneasy relationship that had existed for generations between the village and our neighbour on the hill, though by now more legend than reality, was nevertheless a cause for regret, both to my fellow head and to me. As a raw newcomer, I was deeply indebted to him for practical help during my early days and the friendship that developed from this association led to growing cooperation between the two schools. Beginning with sporting fixtures, in which traces of past rivalry, chiefly on the part of parent spectators, occasionally surfaced, we set about working cooperatively with the older children with the intention of joining forces on a residential field study trip the following summer term.

Until now, the status of our respective schools – my colleague's being a church controlled school, mine a county school – had never been an issue between us. Suddenly, however, this distinction came to the fore. A small one-teacher church school a few miles distant was scheduled to close on the retirement of the headmistress and my colleague and I were requested by the education authority to attend a meeting of parents to outline what our schools had to offer. Anxious to avoid competing with one another, we agreed beforehand on a common approach and maintained this position throughout the meeting. Predictably, most parents had already decided which school they preferred; what saddened us was being involved, albeit unintentionally, in the dividing of a hitherto close-knit community. Fortunately, the increasing level of cooperation between our two schools enabled the affected children to work alongside each other from time to time, which helped to sustain friendships and lessen the impact of the closure of their happy little school.

By rights of course I suppose I should have relished the fact that the school continued to expand. At a time when many village schools were closing through falling numbers, mine was thriving to such an extent that by my sixth year it had become a four-class establishment, with a roll of over a hundred pupils. It should have followed therefore that with the school's long-term future secure and my own teaching duties confined to the top two age groups, I could now settle down to enjoy a less-demanding routine. For various reasons, however, this was not to be. To begin with - and despite the hard work involved – I missed the 'family' atmosphere that I had fostered in the days when I taught the entire junior range. Now, the children entering my class at aged nine had been accustomed to working along more formal lines and a good deal of adjustment was needed before they could benefit from my own mode of working.

In other words, the root of the problem stemmed from the contrasting – and in some cases, conflicting – methods of individual teachers. I sorely missed Pat, my original infants' teacher, whose educational beliefs corresponded more or less with my own. And although I was fortunate eventually in securing a keen and capable young probationer to teach the newly-formed fourth class, the earlier appointment of a member of staff temperamentally unsuited to my approach led to strained relationships and divided loyalties. What I found hard to accept was that in spite of all the fine words and extravagant promises made at interview, it proved unrealistic to expect all members of staff to embrace my entire philosophy and to devote their every waking moment - as I was in danger of doing - exclusively to the life of the school.

I talked the matter over at length with Bill, the area primary adviser, who had by now become a firm friend. We were taking an evening stroll near his home by the banks of the River Windrush, in the hope of seeing his local pair of barn owls. He heard me out patiently before venturing a reply.

'You've somehow got to strike a balance, 'he said at last. 'Much as we strive for perfection, we have to accept that others' priorities lie elsewhere. Try as you will, you can't do it all single-handed. We live in an imperfect world.'

I found myself recalling with a shudder Mr Bacon's warning about the danger of burning myself out. 'I have to compromise my standards – is that what you're saying?' I enquired miserably. My companion gave a sad smile. 'Isn't that what life is all about – compromising?' he mused. 'You've set yourself a high standard and the results are there for all to see. Anyone can see that you love teaching - love it passionately. You are your own man, with your own personal beliefs, and it distresses you that others lack your zest and utter commitment.'

A barn owl - the object of our quest - floated out of the crown of the huge wych elm at our approach and beat its silent moth-like way ahead of us along the river bank. For a moment at least, my immediate concerns took their proper place in a wider perspective.

'As I see it, you have three possible courses of action,' Bill continued, as the ghostly hunter was lost from view round a bend in the river. 'You can accept the plain fact that there is a limit to what you can achieve in your present post, bearing in mind all the circumstances, which are unlikely to change, for the present, anyway. Or you can apply for a smaller school headship, with the uncertainties that would entail, to say nothing of the effect it would have on your long-term career prospects.' He paused, allowing me time to reflect on these options.

'And - the third alternative?' I demanded.

'Go the whole hog.' was the response. 'Start applying for headships of bigger schools. You'd cease to be tied to a class and you'd be able to spread your influence more widely - encourage and guide young teachers along the right path. The path you've taken.' We walked on in silence for some time. My thoughts were in turmoil; were the words of advice given me all those years before by the elderly neighbour who had first suggested I became a teacher - 'Aim high!'– more or less valid now than they had been then ?

'For the record, I'd support your application for a bigger headship wholeheartedly,' my friend said at last. I thanked him for this badly-needed vote of confidence, adding that I now had some hard thinking to do.

Bill's tone changed. 'And while you're exercising the old thought processes, here's something else for you to think about. I'm recruiting a team of valued colleagues to work alongside me, re-training primary teachers in the Gambia during the summer holiday,' he announced. 'Whatever you decide about your future career, I hope you'll see fit to apply.' With my thoughts still in a state of upheaval, my response must have sounded incoherent, to say the least.

'Your application would be a formality,' Bill assured me. 'I want you in the team.'

And so began a new chapter – one that was to have a profound influence on my future life.

Chapter 19

Altogether, I made three six-week visits to The Gambia, all physically and mentally demanding, yet rewarding in the extreme. Until I stepped briefly on to the tarmac at Lisbon airport in the midday heat of a July afternoon in 1969, I had never before set foot on foreign soil. And despite all the preparation that led up to that first tour of duty – Bill's slide talks, background reading, meeting visiting Gambians – nothing could adequately prepare me for the experiences that awaited me in this tiny country - virtually two strips of land, stretching for some 350 miles along either bank of the River Gambia, and sandwiched between two halves of the expansive former French colony of Senegal.

The tours themselves followed the same pattern on each visit. Flying in from our overnight stop in the Canaries, we alighted at the tiny Yundum airport and after passing through a miniature customs post were whisked away for a few days' acclimatisation in the country's one and only de luxe hotel. Here we were pampered with creature comforts; had time to feast our eyes on a dazzling variety of exotic birds and butterflies; and finally subjected to intense late-night briefings that sent us – or me at least – to our mosquito-netted beds in a state of near exhaustion.

And then, after the relaxation, came the reality. I had a dim recollection of Father's *Daily Express* devoting extensive coverage to two failed African agricultural schemes that cost the taxpayer dear in the years following the second world war. The more scandalous - and therefore the more newsworthy - of the two had been a groundnuts scheme in Kenya. The other, as I seemed to recall it, had been known as the Gambia egg scheme, and had involved an unrealistically ambitious project with battery hens. It had never occurred to me to wonder to what use the abandoned battery sheds in that faraway West African colony had been put, following the failure of the ill-conceived venture; now, however, I was about to find out. For the impressively-named Yundum College - The Gambia's sole teacher-training establishment - was in fact that selfsame cluster of buildings, converted now for the mass production of teachers instead of battery eggs. And although the battery cages had long since gone - to be replaced by rickety desks, battered chairs and a few termite-riddled cupboards - there was no mistaking the former use of the rows of identical prefabricated huts, linked by concrete roads, together with the staff bungalows, which were to serve as our living quarters, close by.

Once installed in our accommodation, our first priority was to endeavour to make our lecture rooms welcoming – no easy task considering the drabness, the dirty concrete floors, the intrusion of scavenging mangy-looking dogs, and the relentless heat. Our time was to be divided into two two-week blocs, with each of the four of us tutoring two groups of twenty teachers and with Bill acting in a supervisory role. A few days' break was allowed between the two courses. Fortunately, a plane from an RAF base in the county had flown in crates of books and materials donated by local schools and gradually our barn-like rooms began to resemble the stimulating classrooms we had left behind.

Our daily routine remained the same throughout my three tours. Proceedings opened with all eighty teachers and we four tutors gathering in what served as the college assembly hall to hear Bill's official welcome and introduction to the course. Seated at the front, flanking our leader, we saw before us a sea of eager, expectant faces – chiefly men, but with a scattering of brightly-attired women – who had willingly given up part of their well-earned holiday to return to their former training college to update their teaching techniques.

In our pre-course briefings, Bill had gone to great pains to explain that primary education in The Gambia, as in many emerging African countries, was very much a hit-or-miss affair, with a high percentage of children in the predominantly rural areas, girls especially, receiving little or no schooling whatever. Not only that, but secondary education was reserved for the privileged few who passed a common entrance examination, based on the British model. That in turn meant that primary education had hitherto been geared to a make-or-break exam, a joyless rote-learning system irrelevant and largely incomprehensible to the majority of tribal language-speaking children, whose experience of English was restricted to their time in school.

All this, Bill had explained, was about to change. A country-wide school building programme was being implemented; the hitherto low status of teachers was about to be raised, and an entirely new approach to classroom teaching, - modelled largely on our own county - was being introduced. Our job, in other words, was to equip our groups of teachers for this momentous revolution - a daunting task and a humbling one. Despite Bill's constantly repeated assurances that in giving of our expertise, enthusiasm and respect, we were fulfilling these keen young teachers' most urgent needs, I never lost completely a nagging self-doubt: 'Who am I - from a position of privilege and with the freedom to follow my own dictates without any fear of contradiction - to point the way to these industrious, undervalued colleagues, whose circumstances are a world away from my own?'

Just how appalling were these circumstances was revealed some time later when we drove into the bush to visit remote villages. The sight that met our eyes, even allowing for the schools being closed for the holiday, was demoralising beyond belief; dark, gloomy huts with virtually no furniture or equipment, in which the children had to write in the dust on the floor; schools comprised of roofless areas enclosed by rough wattle screens, lacking any teaching facilities whatever; schools which - though basically sound in structure - had no lockable door and had been invaded by goats, which had devoured or destroyed the children's books.

By contrast, we were taken to see some of the newly-opened 'show' schools, chiefly religious foundations, in which, we were assured, enlightened methods in primary education were already being practised successfully. Following one such visit, to an outstandingly well-built and equipped Roman Catholic primary school, we were invited to dinner by the jocular Irish priest, a man built like a heavyweight boxer, who, it turned out, was something of an authority on Gambian wild life. After a sumptuous meal, prepared and served by a retinue of servants, we retired to the veranda of his bungalow in the fleeting dusk, to listen to his stories, told in a rich Irish brogue, with a background of African night sounds.

Suddenly, out of the corner of my eye, I caught sight of a creature resembling a giant woodlouse, making its way determinedly along the edge of the veranda. Following my rapt gaze, our host paused in mid-flow, reached for a large ash tray and inverting it over the beast, promised that we would examine it after he had finished his story. Predictably, one tale led to another and by the time he paused for breath, some time later, the ash tray, propelled by its hidden captive, had moved several feet along the veranda. The giant woodlouse proved to be just one of many fascinating creatures we encountered on our travels. We had already become familiar with geckos and preying mantis in our lecture rooms; monitor lizards shinning up the drainpipes of our bungalows and gaudy butterflies as large as saucers flitting lazily in the college grounds. And although big cats had virtually disappeared from the Gambian bush, their lesser brethren, the serval and the civet, were still to be seen, though all too often as captives or as pathetic skins on market stalls.

But it was the birds that provided The Gambia's main wildlife attraction. I spent every spare minute feasting my senses on the wealth of colourful species everywhere around, ranging from diminutive sunbirds to kingfishers, waders, herons, hawks and vultures, constantly adding a new and unfamiliar sighting to my list.

By the time of my final tour, in 1975, change in many forms had taken place in The Gambia. The advances in primary education were evident for all to see and the pay and conditions of the teachers had improved correspondingly. Tourism, in its infancy on my earlier visits, was expanding rapidly, with hotels springing up along the hitherto empty and pristine coastline. Sadly, this transformation had its inevitable side-effects – commercialism, prostitution, a drift from the land – that threatened the country's social fabric.

By then, too, my own life had also changed. I had bid farewell to my Cotswold village school and moved to a larger one, not far distant. And so I remained – and remain still – a Derbyshire man in self-imposed exile, settled contentedly in this other, beautiful corner of England, yet fondly recalling my native county, its splendid scenery - and in a way that defies logic, its long- abandoned pits and the men alongside whom I worked – that shaped my early years and in so doing laid claim to a lifetime's loyalty.

End

Also by Gordon Ottewell

Square Peg: Memoirs of a Misfit Miner
Discovering Cotswold Villages
Literary Strolls in the Cotswolds & Forest of Dean
Gloucestershire Countryside
Theme walks in Gloucestershire
150 miles of Gloucestershire
The Evenlode: An exploration of a Cotswold river
Family walks in the Cotswolds
Family walks around Stratford & Banbury
Wildlife walks in the north Cotswolds
A Cotswold Country Diary
Literary Strolls in Wiltshire & Somerset
Walking in haunted Gloucestershire (with F.E. Jackson)
Warde Fowler's Countryside (edited)

For children
Journey from Darkness
Tangleton

Acknowledgement

As with 'Square Peg', the first volume of my memoirs, this book would never have seen the light of day but for the invaluable encouragement and expertise of my friend Robert Talbot, to whom I owe an immense debt of gratitude.

Gordon Ottewell